QuickBooks

The Illustrated Step-by-Step Guide to Stress-Free Bookkeeping for Small Business Owner

Lincoln Griffin

Table of Content

Introduction

Welcome to a journey of financial mastery with QuickBooks, a sojourn through the realms of fiscal wisdom. Imagine standing at the threshold of a vast library, each book a repository of knowledge waiting to unfurl before you. This chapter is the inviting corridor, the archway that ushers you into a world where numbers dance and figures speak the language of growth. Here, we prepare to embark on a quest not just to learn, but to transform our relationship with the tools that forge the backbone of business. With every page, we'll weave understanding into the fabric of our daily practices, and with every concept grasped, we move closer to financial fluency and confidence.

Why This Book is Different

Embarking on the journey of financial fluency can often resemble the daunting task of learning a new language – one that's peppered with jargon, intricate rules, and the intimidating repercussions of miscommunication. Many volumes that aim to be your guide through the thicket of accounting software like QuickBooks offer either a rudimentary overview or a dive that's so deep, you might feel the need for a lifeline just to navigate the table of contents.

Here's where this book plants its flag firmly in the ground – it is crafted not just as a manual, but as a compass that points you in the right direction when you're lost in the labyrinth of ledgers and liabilities. It distinguishes itself by not just showing you the what, but intricately detailing the why and the how in a manner that speaks directly to the heart of entrepreneurs who breathe the air of innovation and efficiency.

We begin by setting the stage with the unvarnished truth: accounting isn't just about keeping score; it's about storytelling. Your business's financial records narrate the tale of where you've been, where you stand, and where you're headed, in the stark dialect of dollars and cents. This book aims to be your Rosetta Stone, translating the dense dialect of accounting into actionable insights.

So why is this book different? Because it's been designed with the understanding that each entrepreneur is different. Your challenges are unique, your time is valuable, and your relationship with numbers is personal. You're not looking for a textbook – you're searching for a conversation with someone who's been in the trenches, who's felt the frustration of balancing a budget at midnight, and who knows that every minute spent fumbling with finances is a minute not spent on innovation.

It approaches QuickBooks not just as a tool, but as an ally. Throughout its pages, this book acknowledges the cold sweat that breaks out when you hit a snag in reconciling accounts, or the sense of triumph when your quarterly reports align like a symphony. It's written with an empathy that stems from shared experience, for it's penned by authors who have navigated the same journey you're on, armed with the same tools you're using.

Moreover, this guide reaches beyond the mere mechanics of QuickBooks and delves into the philosophy of financial management. It understands that your relationship with this software is akin to a partnership – where your input and its processing capabilities must dance in sync. And for those moments when you find your business rhythm disrupted by a misstep in accounting, this book steps in as your dance instructor, your guide to getting back in step without missing a beat.

Instead of showering you with step-by-step instructions that lead you down a path with blinders on, this narrative seeks to widen your perspective, to help you understand the underlying structure and logic. It encourages you not just to follow instructions but to see through them, to predict them, and ultimately, to create a financial strategy that's tailored to your business DNA.

Consider for a moment the story of Tech-Savvy Tim – our archetype for a modern entrepreneur. Tim's tale is one that echoes across many a startup office and co-working space. He's the visionary who can code a solution to any problem, whose brain works in algorithms and efficiency, yet who finds himself perplexed by the persistent complexities of QuickBooks. This book reaches out to Tim, and many others like him, with a lifeline woven from understanding, experience, and the genuine desire to empower.

It shuns the repetition of concepts you've encountered a hundred times in favor of fresh insights and novel strategies. It eschews the mechanical march through features and functions to explore the soul of QuickBooks – how it can serve not just as your accounting software, but as a barometer for your business's financial health.

In essence, this book is different because it is alive with the knowledge that the essence of accounting – the very heartbeat of QuickBooks – is not in its ability to crunch numbers, but in its power to crystallize your vision into tangible results. It's here to help you turn the mundane task of accounting into a strategic powerhouse, driving growth, forecasting trends, and breathing life into the story that you are bold enough to write for your business.

So, as you turn these pages, know that they are not just filled with words, but with understanding. They don't just teach; they guide. And they don't just inform; they transform. Welcome to a new chapter in your entrepreneurial journey, one where QuickBooks is not a chore, but a chapter in your success story waiting to be written.

Who Should Read This Book

Imagine standing at the crossroads of innovation and organization, where the map in your hand is drawn in figures and financial forecasts. Here, the horizon is broad and the path forward is paved with the potential for profit, but only if you can decode the signs along the way. This book is for those who find themselves at this juncture, irrespective of the industry, from the artisans of commerce to the architects of technology. It is written for the intrepid souls who've realized that understanding the ledger beneath the legend of their business ventures is not just beneficial, but essential.

If you're the entrepreneur who has faced the tempest of term sheets and the intricacies of investment rounds, this book speaks to you. It's for the small business owner who pours their passion into products and services, who knows their customers by name, and who is now poised to know their accounts with the same intimacy. The fledgling founder, whose business plan is as much a work of art as a spreadsheet, will find here a kindred spirit that offers guidance without condescension.

This book also extends its hand to the self-taught, the self-starters, and the self-employed. It acknowledges the web developer who bootstrapped their way to a bespoke business, the freelance designer whose creativity is boundless but who seeks to bind their financials with equal flair. It is a tome for the consultant who crafts strategies for clients with ease but finds the fiscal architecture of their own enterprise a labyrinth more complex than the problems they solve for others.

And what of the managers and executives, those seasoned navigators of commerce who steer the ship but have yet to master the currents of QuickBooks? To them, this book offers a lighthouse – a beacon designed to illuminate the depths and dangers of accounting software, ensuring that the voyage through fiscal waters is one of discovery, not despair. It stands as a companion to the corporate leader who understands that to truly command the helm, they must also be adept at reading the financial stars above.

Let us also speak to the accountants and bookkeepers, the unsung heroes in the annals of any business saga. This book is an ode to your craft, an acknowledgment that while the principles of accounting are timeless, the tools are ever-evolving. It invites you to explore QuickBooks not just as a software but as a symphony – to bring your expertise to its keyboard and compose financial statements that sing with clarity and vision.

The non-profit steward, too, will discover wisdom within these pages. Here lies a recognition of the unique challenges you face, where every dollar saved is a service secured, every report a testament to transparency and trust. This book does not overlook the fact that within the noble pursuit of your mission lies the need for a practical understanding of practical software.

In this book, teachers will find a resource as well. The economics professor who seeks to bring the real world into the classroom, the vocational instructor who equips minds with the skills for commerce, and the mentor who guides startups in incubators – all will find in this book a source of wisdom to be imparted to eager learners.

And we must not forget the students, the bright-eyed aspirants to business acumen. If you are the student who has traded theoretical knowledge for the trenches of a trial balance, this narrative is your textbook for the real world. It seeks to escort you from the halls of academia into the bustling streets of commerce with confidence and competence in QuickBooks.

In the spirit of inclusivity, this book also addresses those who find themselves inadvertently thrust into the financial realm. The artist who finds that their passion project has grown into a profitable endeavor, the engineer who's patented a process and now must patent a path through the world of business – you will find solace and strategy within these pages.

It's important to say that this book does not draw lines or boundaries; it does not set prerequisites of knowledge or experience. It is a welcoming hearth for anyone who has ever felt the heat of uncertainty when opening QuickBooks. It's a testament to the belief that with the right guide, financial software can become a canvas, not just a calculator, for anyone with a dream and the drive to pursue it.

To distill it down to the essence, this book is for the curious, the courageous, and the committed – for anyone who's ever stood before the vast sea of their business's finances and wished for a navigator to chart the course. It's for those who know that in the world of business, the only constant is change, and the best way to manage that change is to understand the language it speaks.

As you read on, you may see yourself reflected in the examples and narratives that are woven into the fabric of this book. They are there to remind you that this is not just a journey through QuickBooks; it is a journey through the collective experiences of those who have charted these waters before you. It is a book that speaks not just to the mind, but to the spirit of enterprise that lives within us all.

How to Use This Book

Embark on this literary voyage with the intention to explore, not merely to arrive at a destination. This book is constructed not as a sequence of rigid steps but as a pathway where each reader may wander, may wonder, and, indeed, may find their own rhythm as they traverse the pages. To read this book is to engage in a dialogue, not with a voice that dictates, but with one that suggests, that questions, that leads gently toward enlightenment.

Approach each chapter as you would a conversation with a wise friend. The text is crafted to be a discourse that invites reflection, beckons questions, and fosters an environment where learning is not a solitary endeavor but a shared journey. Permit yourself the liberty to pause, to ponder, to peruse again passages that resonate or challenge. The wisdom here is not a monologue to be hurried through; it is a narrative to be absorbed, a tapestry woven from the threads of understanding and application.

Consider your practical engagement with QuickBooks as a canvas, and this book as your palette of techniques and insights. The chapters are not mere instructions; they are the hues and shades of proficiency you will blend on the canvas of your financial undertakings. Use this book as an artist uses a color wheel—not in a prescribed order, but as inspiration strikes, as the picture you are painting requires depth here or contrast there.

Allow the anecdotes and stories within to act as allegories, mirrors in which you may see your own experiences reflected. These tales are not mere diversions; they are the embodiment of theory, the life breathed into concepts, the humanity interwoven with technology. They serve to remind that QuickBooks is not an abstract concept dwelling in the digital ether but a tool crafted by humans, for humans.

This book, with its rich narrative and conversational wisdom, also serves as a guide to self-discovery. As you delve into the pages, you will encounter exercises and thought experiments designed to reveal not just the capacities of QuickBooks but also the contours of your own understanding. They are stepping stones across the river of knowledge, placed not at regular intervals, but just where you might need to pivot or leap to continue your passage.

Engage with this book as you would with the map of an unknown city. The chapters are neighborhoods, each with its own character and secrets to be discovered. Some you will visit out of necessity, to learn the lay of the land; others will catch your eye with their charm and pull you into their streets. Wander these textual precincts with curiosity, and you will find that understanding QuickBooks becomes less about following directions and more about building a mental model of the city of commerce.

This book is not a monolith, but a mosaic, a compilation of fragments each complete in itself but part of a greater whole. It eschews the linear in favor of the organic, understanding that learning is a process as varied as the individuals undertaking it. Some readers will move cover to cover, others will jump between chapters as need or interest dictates. Both approaches are valid, for the goal is not to finish but to grow, to expand the boundaries of what you know and can do.

Treat this book as you would a mentor's advice—available when you need it, always ready to offer insight, but never overbearing. Keep it at your side as you work with QuickBooks, allowing its chapters to inform your actions without compelling them. The insights within are not edicts but suggestions, the gentle guidance of a teacher whose satisfaction comes from the student's achievement, not adherence to doctrine.

This book also serves as a compass in the wilderness of financial management. It is designed to help you navigate, to orient you when you feel lost, to provide a true north when the way forward is obscured by doubt or complexity. It is, at its core, a testament to the belief that anyone can master the tools necessary to sculpt their financial fate, given the right guidance.

It is my hope that as you use this book, you will come to see QuickBooks not as an adversary to be conquered but as an ally to be understood and befriended. The pages within are not barriers to be overcome but stepping stones, and each step is one taken not alone but in the good company of a guide who has traversed this path many times before.

In the end, the manner in which you use this book should mirror your unique journey through the world of business and finance. There is no one right way to read these pages, just as there is no one right way to achieve success. The path you chart through this book is yours alone to draw, a route that is as individual as your aspirations, as bespoke as your dreams.

Let this be the beginning of a conversation that continues beyond the final page, a discourse that becomes part of your daily practice with QuickBooks. As you weave the advice, the anecdotes, and the practical wisdom of this book into your routine, may you find that you are not just using a tool, but mastering an art—the art of financial finesse.

So, read not just with your eyes but with your mind wide open. Use this book not just as a source of answers but as a springboard for questions. Apply its wisdom not mechanically, but with the creativity and passion that is the hallmark of all great endeavors. And may your journey with QuickBooks, guided by these pages, be as rewarding as it is enlightening.

Part I: Getting Started with QuickBooks

Chapter 1: QuickBooks: An Overview

Welcome to the gateway of mastery over your financial narratives, where the realms of QuickBooks' offerings are unveiled. At the heart of American ingenuity and entrepreneurial spirit, QuickBooks stands as the stalwart ally to the ambitious microbusiness owner. This chapter unfolds the story of QuickBooks, an accounting beacon illuminating the path to fiscal clarity and control for the smallest of enterprises. Herein lies a detailed exploration of its origins, its pivotal role in the fabric of American business, and a comparative analysis of its diverse incarnations, all tailored to fit the unique needs of U.S. entrepreneurs.

What is QuickBooks?

Introduction to QuickBooks as the Leading Accounting Software for U.S. Small Businesses

In the dynamic expanse of U.S. commerce, where the spirit of entrepreneurship beats with vibrant tenacity, QuickBooks stands not merely as a software but as an emblem of financial coherence and clarity. Its inception was less about fanfare and more a whispered promise into the ears of diligent business owners craving simplicity amidst the labyrinthine complexities of financial management. This section unfolds the narrative of QuickBooks, examining its ascendancy to becoming the touchstone of accounting software for the country's industrious small businesses.

Imagine a tool that doesn't just perform a function but transforms a process. QuickBooks, in its essence, is just that— a transformative agent that has shifted the paradigm from pen-and-paper drudgery to sleek, seamless digital efficiency. For the legions of U.S. small businesses, it is the champion of their financial narratives, turning novices into maestros of their monetary symphonies. This is not about the software in isolation but about its symbiotic relationship with the heartbeat of American enterprise.

To understand QuickBooks is to appreciate its evolution as a responsive entity that has, over the years, become intricately woven into the fabric of small business operations. It began as a response to a gap, a void in the market where small businesses grappled with accounting software that was either too rudimentary or excessively complex. In this gap, QuickBooks found its calling, morphing into a platform that struck an exquisite balance between sophistication and user-friendliness.

This segment of the chapter is a deep dive into the ethos behind QuickBooks, illuminating its design philosophy that embraces accessibility without compromising on power and versatility. It's a tale of unceasing refinement and a testament to the enduring commitment to support the backbone of the American economy—small businesses. Here, we explore how QuickBooks has steadfastly held the position of the preeminent accounting software by staying attuned to the changing tides of technological advancement and the undulating demands of its users.

QuickBooks did not become a leader in a vacuum; its ascendancy is interlaced with stories of businesses that have burgeoned under its aegis. It mirrors the entrepreneurial journey, from fledgling start-ups to established enterprises, capturing the essence of American industriousness. Each feature, each tool within QuickBooks has been crafted with the acute awareness of an entrepreneur's journey, designed not just to track and manage finances but to elevate the business process to a plane of strategic insight and foresight.

As we peel back the layers, we find QuickBooks isn't just a product but a reflection of a broader economic narrative, a chronicle of resilience and adaptability that resonates with the ethos of the American dream. Through its intuitive interface, it has democratized financial management, enabling businesses of all sizes to harness the power of their financial data to drive decision-making and foster growth.

Within this expanse, QuickBooks has carved out a space where numbers do more than add up—they tell a story, a saga of growth, challenges, triumphs, and the relentless pursuit of excellence. It is here that we embark on a journey through the features and functions of QuickBooks, understanding how it has become an indispensable ally to U.S. small businesses, an ally that speaks the language of both the layman and the expert with equal fluency.

The following narrative does not merely dissect QuickBooks as a software solution but celebrates it as an enduring legacy in the American business landscape. It is an ode to the quintessential blend of simplicity and power, a harmonious intersection where ease of use meets the robust demands of small business accounting. As we traverse through this exploration, we bear witness to how QuickBooks has emerged as the leading light, guiding businesses through the fog of financial uncertainty to a harbor of fiscal clarity and control.

Let us, therefore, embark on this enlightening expedition with a sense of curiosity and an appetite for understanding, as we delve into the core of what makes QuickBooks the quintessential companion for U.S. small businesses in the realm of accounting—a realm where QuickBooks has become not just a tool, but a transformative experience, shaping the financial landscapes of small businesses with precision, insight, and intuitive grace.

The Evolution of QuickBooks in the American Market: Adapting to Small Business Needs

QuickBooks' odyssey through the American market is a narrative of relentless innovation and adaptation—a continuum that mirrors the ever-evolving landscape of U.S. small businesses. Its story is one of transformation, a journey punctuated by a series of pivotal shifts and turns, responding to the burgeoning needs of an entrepreneurial class that forms the bedrock of the American economy.

In the nascent days of desktop computing, small business owners found themselves wading through the quagmire of financial management with rudimentary tools that bore the imprint of a pre-digital epoch. Enter QuickBooks, a harbinger of change that emerged from the digital ether, offering a lifeline to those awash in a sea of financial complexity. Its arrival was more than just the introduction of a new software—it was the dawn of a new age in small business finance management.

As we chart the trajectory of QuickBooks, we see an evolution that is inextricably linked to the heartbeat of small businesses—their needs, their growth, and their unyielding spirit of innovation. It is an evolution characterized by a series of metamorphoses, each iteration of QuickBooks more perceptive, more intuitive, and more attuned to the pulse of small business America.

The inception of QuickBooks was met with a groundswell of approval from business owners who found solace in its simplicity and power. Yet, the creators were not content to rest on their laurels. With the tenacity of visionaries, they forged ahead, sculpting QuickBooks into an ever more refined instrument of financial clarity. As the market burgeoned with new businesses, each with its unique array of needs and challenges, QuickBooks evolved, its features expanding and deepening, its interface becoming ever more streamlined.

In this unfolding saga, we see QuickBooks as a reflection of American ingenuity, a testament to the ethos of perpetual improvement. With each update, with each leap forward, QuickBooks has demonstrated an uncanny ability to anticipate and respond to the shifting paradigms of the marketplace. It has morphed from a static piece of software into a dynamic ecosystem, one that embraces the cloud, mobile technology, and artificial intelligence to offer more than just accounting solutions—it offers a comprehensive suite of tools that empower small businesses to take command of their financial destiny.

The evolution of QuickBooks is also the story of its user base, a diverse tapestry of entrepreneurs who have found in this software a partner for their journey. From the local bakery that has been a community staple for generations to the tech startup that dreams of revolutionizing their industry, QuickBooks has adapted to fit the contours of their needs, ensuring that its capabilities are not just sophisticated, but accessible and relevant.

It is within this context that QuickBooks' ability to adapt shines brightest. The software's developers have cultivated an intimate dialogue with its users, ensuring that feedback and real-world usage inform the evolution of the platform. This has fostered an environment where QuickBooks is not just used but engaged with, where its development is a collaborative dance between the creators and the community.

As businesses grapple with the demands of an ever-accelerating world, QuickBooks has not just kept pace but has often led the charge, introducing features that harness the full potential of the digital age. It has integrated seamlessly with a myriad of other services and platforms, understanding that in the tapestry of small business operations, financial management is but one thread interwoven with many others.

The journey of QuickBooks is also a chronicle of education and empowerment. By demystifying the complexities of accounting, it has given rise to a new generation of entrepreneurs who approach the financial aspects of their businesses with confidence and clarity. It has fostered a sense of ownership over financial data, providing insights that drive smarter business decisions and strategies.

In the chapters that follow, we will delve deeper into the tangible manifestations of this evolution. We will explore the iterations of QuickBooks, the enhancements and innovations that have solidified its standing in the marketplace. We will recount the stories of businesses that have grown in tandem with QuickBooks, their successes and challenges woven into the larger narrative of this platform's development.

QuickBooks' journey is far from complete. As the horizon of technology expands, so too will the capabilities and reach of this storied software. It stands poised at the edge of tomorrow, ready to evolve in lockstep with the American small business, ready to meet the future with the same blend of simplicity and power that has been its hallmark from the very beginning.

In this spirit, we embark on an exploration of QuickBooks' evolutionary path—a path characterized by foresight, adaptability, and an unyielding commitment to the small businesses that are the lifeblood of the American market. It is a journey that speaks not only to the capabilities of QuickBooks but to the indomitable spirit of those it serves, a narrative that continues to unfold with each passing day.

QuickBooks Desktop vs QuickBooks Online

Comparison of Features: Which is Best for the U.S. Entrepreneur?

The quintessential quandary that entrepreneurs in the U.S. grapple with when considering QuickBooks is not just about choosing accounting software; it is about choosing the right confidant for their financial narrative. QuickBooks Desktop and QuickBooks Online are not mere variants but embodiments of different philosophies tailored to divergent entrepreneurial journeys. This exploration is a tale of two platforms, each with a distinct heartbeat, each resonating with the unique pulse of American entrepreneurship.

QuickBooks Desktop, a stalwart of financial management, has long been the bedrock upon which many U.S. businesses have built their accounting practices. It is a bastion of reliability, a system that has evolved over years but has retained the core of its initial promise: robustness and comprehensive control. The Desktop version is akin to a seasoned financial counselor, offering depth, detail, and a sense of solidity. Its myriad features are crafted like the many-leveled basements of a skyscraper—secure, vast, and designed to anchor even the most complex of financial structures.

For the entrepreneur whose business is an intricate tapestry of transactions requiring meticulous detail and customization, QuickBooks Desktop offers a canvas as expansive as the American dream itself. It provides the tools to craft a financial portrait with the precision of an artisan, offering features that allow for detailed inventory management, complex job costing, and multi-faceted reporting. This platform speaks the language of the hands-on entrepreneur, the individual who desires close proximity to the levers of financial control, who takes solace in the tangibility of data living securely within their own infrastructure.

On the flip side of the coin, or perhaps the cloud, is QuickBooks Online—a beacon of connectivity and flexibility. In a world where business is not anchored to a desk but moves with the fluidity of the digital age, QuickBooks Online is a testament to freedom and accessibility. It is the embodiment of financial management on-the-go, a companion as mobile as the entrepreneur who seeks to transcend the confines of the office. Its architecture is not of brick and mortar but of bits and bytes, offering real-time access to financial data, collaborative tools, and an ecosystem of integrations that breathe connectivity into every transaction.

For the business owner whose operations are a stream rather than a lake, whose needs call for access over containment, QuickBooks Online is the vessel that sails the currents of commerce with agility. It aligns with the beat of the urban freelancer, the rural artisan, and the suburban startup by offering a platform that is both a lens to view financial health and a window to the future of business mobility. Its continuous updates, cloud-based data backups, and collaborative capabilities are the fibers of a financial web that captures the essence of modern business operations.

Yet, the decision is not one to be made lightly, nor is it a binary between tradition and innovation. The U.S. entrepreneur must weigh the scales of features, understanding that each business is a living entity with unique demands and aspirations. QuickBooks Desktop and QuickBooks Online are not competitors but complements in the QuickBooks family, each suited to different life stages and business strategies.

The entrepreneur must ask: does the business require the robustness and specific functionalities of Desktop, or the anytime-anywhere accessibility of Online? Is the preference for a one-time purchase and localized data storage, or is it towards a subscription model with cloud-based fluidity? These questions are not merely operational but philosophical, for the choice of accounting software is a reflection of the business identity itself.

In making this decision, one must consider the granularity of feature sets. QuickBooks Desktop, for instance, may boast a superior suite of tools for businesses that require detailed inventory tracking and prefer a hands-on approach to financial management. With its ability to track hundreds of thousands of customers, vendors, and inventory items, it stands as a veritable fortress of capability.

Conversely, QuickBooks Online is the maestro of convenience and collaborative possibilities. Its ability to connect with a plethora of apps and services streamlines operations, making it an ideal choice for businesses that thrive on integration and real-time collaboration. With its automated updates and cloud-based ecosystem, QuickBooks Online is an enabler of financial management that is as dynamic as the marketplace it serves.

As the narrative unfolds, each platform reveals its character through its features. QuickBooks Desktop might offer a more extensive list of reports, more customization options, and a greater sense of control for the entrepreneur who revels in the granular aspects of their business's financial story. QuickBooks Online, with its intuitive design and ease of use, may appeal to the entrepreneur who values flexibility and instant connectivity over the complexity of features.

This chapter does not seek to prescribe but to enlighten, offering a panoramic view of QuickBooks' offerings tailored to the diverse tapestry of U.S. entrepreneurship. The aim is not to direct but to inform, to provide the U.S. entrepreneur with the insight necessary to choose the QuickBooks variant that best harmonizes with their business symphony.

The forthcoming pages will not dictate but guide, providing a narrative of features, benefits, and the quintessential elements that define QuickBooks Desktop and QuickBooks Online. It is a journey through the capabilities of each, a journey that each entrepreneur must undertake armed with the knowledge of their own business's heart and horizon.

As this exposition concludes, remember that the choice between QuickBooks Desktop and QuickBooks Online is more than a mere selection of product—it is a reflection of your business strategy, operational needs, and personal philosophy towards financial management. It is a significant chapter in the larger story of your entrepreneurial venture, one that demands careful consideration and an understanding of the long-term narrative of your business's growth and evolution. Choose wisely, for the platform you select will become the financial bedrock upon which your business's story will be written.

Subscription Models in the U.S.: Costs and Scalability for Microbusinesses

In the bustling corridors of American commerce, the lifeblood of the economy pumps through the veins of microbusinesses. It's within these small but mighty enterprises that QuickBooks has planted its roots, offering a subscription model that is not merely a pricing strategy but a partnership for growth. The intricacy of this model lies not just in its cost structure but in its capacity to scale with the aspirations of these businesses, to stretch as they expand, and to accommodate the undulating tides of market demand.

Embarking upon the QuickBooks subscription journey, the microbusiness in the U.S. encounters a path that is both enlightening and daunting. The pricing models are not carved in stone but etched in water, fluid and adaptable to the needs of burgeoning businesses. Each subscription tier is not a rung on a ladder but a gateway to new possibilities, a stepping stone to a future where financial clarity and control are not just desired but demanded.

The cost of QuickBooks subscriptions whispers tales of investment and return, of expenditures that bear fruit over time. The commitment to a QuickBooks subscription is not an expenditure but an investment in a company's future financial integrity. It's akin to hiring a silent accountant, one who works tirelessly, demanding nothing but the monthly tribute of a subscription fee. For the microbusiness, this fee is a figure woven into the fabric of their operational expenses, one that must be measured against the tapestry of services rendered.

QuickBooks Online, with its subscription-based heart, beats in rhythm with the pace of the U.S. microbusiness. This heartbeat is a metric of flexibility, offering tiers that cater to the minimalist needs of the solo entrepreneur and the more expansive requirements of a small team poised for growth. The structure of these tiers reflects an understanding of diversity in business operations, acknowledging that not all microbusinesses are birthed equal, nor do they yearn for identical tools from their accounting software.

The scalability of QuickBooks subscriptions is a narrative of growth, reflecting the journey of a microbusiness from its nascent stage to its zenith. As the business flourishes, so too can the subscription evolve, ascending through tiers as the company's needs become more sophisticated. This scalability is not just a feature but a lifeline for microbusinesses, ensuring that their financial management tools can keep pace with their progress, expanding in capability as the business sprawls in scope and complexity.

Yet, the considerations of cost and scalability intertwine like strands of DNA, each a vital component of the decision-making matrix. The microbusiness must navigate this matrix with foresight, projecting future needs against the backdrop of current financial constraints. The QuickBooks subscription model is a beacon in this matrix, guiding businesses through the fog of pricing structures with transparency and a keen sense of partnership.

The dialogue of subscription costs is not a monologue but a conversation between QuickBooks and the microbusiness, a discourse that revolves around value, not just dollars and cents. It's a conversation that addresses the qualitative aspect of features, the security of cloud storage, the assurance of support, and the promise of continuous updates. These qualitative elements are not additional benefits but foundational pillars upon which the QuickBooks subscription model stands firm.

The entrepreneur pondering the QuickBooks subscription is presented with a panorama of potential. They are tasked with choosing not just a price but a pathway, one that will shepherd their financial data through the labyrinth of business operations. Each subscription tier offers a different vantage point, a different set of tools that can map the terrain of their business landscape with increasing detail and depth.

Delving into the financial alchemy of QuickBooks subscriptions, the microbusiness finds a spectrum of options. From simple income and expense tracking to advanced reporting and analytics, the choice of subscription level must mirror the sophistication of the business's financial narrative. The tiers are akin to layers in a geode, each revealing more complexity and beauty as one delves deeper, each offering a richer view of the business's fiscal health.

As the journey through the subscription models unfolds, it becomes clear that QuickBooks has not just built a pricing ladder but a pricing ecosystem. This ecosystem thrives on the principles of adaptability and partnership, ensuring that as the microbusiness in the U.S. pivots, scales, and evolves, so too will its accounting solutions. The QuickBooks subscription is not a static entity but a living component of the business, one that breathes in tandem with its growth and adapts to its changing needs.

In conclusion, the QuickBooks subscription model is not merely a choice but a strategic decision for the U.S. microbusiness. It is a decision that marries the financial present with the future, ensuring that as the business weaves its narrative in the American market, its accounting platform will be a steadfast companion, not just in cost but in scalable value. The subscription models offered by QuickBooks are not just tiers but testimonies to the commitment to grow alongside the microbusinesses that form the backbone of the American economy.

Chapter 2: Setting Up Your QuickBooks Account

Embarking on the QuickBooks journey signals a pivotal step for the American business owner, one that aligns financial processes with the vibrant pulse of commerce and industry. This chapter serves as a guiding beacon, illuminating the path through the initial setup—a customized foundation built to uphold the intricacies of your entrepreneurial endeavor. As you sift through the pages, you'll uncover the critical company information required to anchor your business in compliance and best practices, while configuring settings to resonate with the unique cadence of your market. The setup process is not merely about entering data; it's about weaving the financial fabric that will support your business's growth, sustainability, and adaptability in the dynamic economic arena of the United States.

Step-by-Step Setup

Initial Setup: A Guide Tailored to the American Business Owner

Embarking on the financial journey of a business, the American entrepreneur seeks a companion in technology that echoes the spirit of enterprise and ingenuity - a role QuickBooks is primed to fill. The initial setup of this software is not merely about pressing buttons and toggling settings; it's about laying down the digital cornerstone of one's business empire, brick by meticulous brick.

Picture the scene: a business owner, brimming with aspirations, is poised at the threshold of opportunity. With the commencement of the QuickBooks setup process, they are not simply firing up a program; they're igniting a narrative of success, carefully curated to comply with the intricate tapestry of U.S. regulations and market demands.

The genesis of this setup journey requires a dialogue with the software, a conversation punctuated by the entrepreneur's vision and the realities of the market. This stage is where ambition meets method, where the lofty goals of the entrepreneur are distilled into the concrete elements of data and numbers. One begins with the basics - the business type, structure, and industry. Each choice is a step toward clarity, a nod to the complex landscape of American business legislation.

As the process unfolds, the entrepreneur is asked to etch in the name of their endeavor - perhaps chosen with hope or perhaps a tribute to a legacy. This name will soon headline invoices, champion financial reports, and stand tall in the bustling marketplace. Next, a flurry of details that form the backbone of fiscal identity - the EIN, the actual structure be it LLC, sole proprietorship, or corporation, the business addresses both physical and virtual.

The software, akin to a seasoned guide, ushers the entrepreneur through the financial maze of account charts, meticulously mapping out the economic territory that the business will navigate. This is no cookie-cutter expedition; it is bespoke, crafted to accommodate the unique financial dialect spoken by the American small business sector.

QuickBooks, with its sophisticated arsenal of tools, ensures that even the most unseasoned business owner is shielded from the labyrinthine complexity of financial setup. It renders the opaque transparent, turning what could be an odyssey of administrative burden into a streamlined path toward operational readiness.

What follows is a dance of digits - inputting the start date of the business, the fiscal year's commencement, and the intricate web of initial balances. Here lies the groundwork of history, the financial footprints that have led to this moment of new beginnings. The entrepreneur, in this act, is not just inputting numbers; they're scribing the prelude to their business story.

This initial encounter with QuickBooks is a rite of passage for the business owner, one that is recognized by the software's intuitive design - guiding, not goading, towards financial eloquence. The outcome of this setup is a symphony of systems, a harmonized suite of features ready to embark on the business odyssey that is uniquely American in its rhythm and pace.

In the hands of QuickBooks, the complexities of accounting become an orchestra of opportunity, poised to elevate the quintessential American business from nascent dreams to tangible success.

Essential Company Information to Input for U.S. Compliance

In the realm of American enterprise, compliance is not just a statutory mandate; it is the rhythm that synchronizes the symphony of business activities. QuickBooks, acting as the maestro for this symphony, understands the intricacies of this rhythm. The essential company information you input is the score from which your business's fiscal performance will be judged.

Engraving your company's identity within QuickBooks begins with more than just a name. It's a ceremonial etching of your business's essence into the annals of the U.S. economic system. This is where you lay out the contours of your business's tax landscape, shaping how the terrains of compliance will be navigated.

Inputting your Employer Identification Number (EIN) is akin to giving your business its own social security number, a unique identifier in the bustling metropolis of commerce. This number speaks to government entities; it's a silent yet potent communicator of your business's legitimacy and readiness to align with the federal tapestry of taxation.

When it comes to the structure of your company—whether it be LLC, S-Corp, C-Corp, or sole proprietorship—QuickBooks does not merely ask for a label. It seeks to understand the skeleton of your venture, how its bones are connected to uphold the weight of fiscal responsibilities.

The physical address you input is not just a location; it's a beacon for state and local tax implications. QuickBooks takes this information and sculpts the tax portrait, tailored to the precise geolocation of your operations. As you delineate the boundaries of your business domicile, QuickBooks absorbs this data, preparing to wrestle with the nexus of state-specific tax laws on your behalf.

But it's not just about the skeletal framework of compliance; it's also about the flesh and blood of day-to-day operations. You will furnish details that define the financial health of your enterprise: the start dates, the bank account numbers that act as the lifelines of your cash flow, and the credit arrangements that will fuel your growth.

Every dollar is accounted for as you enter the beginning balances of your accounts. QuickBooks, with its algorithmic prowess, transforms these figures into a prologue of your financial narrative, setting the stage for the chapters of economic storytelling that will unfold.

The chart of accounts is where you paint the canvas of your company's financial identity. Each account, be it for assets, liabilities, equity, revenue, or expenses, is a stroke of the brush that defines the shades and textures of your economic portrait.

Liabilities, those fiscal obligations that your company will shoulder, are entered with precision, ensuring that every forthcoming transaction adheres to the stringent codes of U.S. accounting principles. These entries are not merely numbers; they are the embodiment of promises made by your business to creditors, partners, and stakeholders.

When it comes to assets, QuickBooks becomes the custodian of their value, vigilantly tracking their ebb and flow through the tides of your business operations. The commitments and revenues, the lifeforce of your enterprise, are entered with foresight, with an understanding that these numbers will ebb and swell with the health of your trade.

Through this meticulous ritual of information input, your company's compliance posture is fortified. QuickBooks becomes the guardian of your fiscal integrity, a watchful sentry standing at the gates of regulatory adherence. The software is an extension of your entrepreneurial spirit, meshed with the precision of a calculator and the insight of a sage advisor.

As the final bits of data are woven into the QuickBooks tapestry, a clear image emerges—one of a business standing tall and confident, its compliance armor gleaming under the scrutiny of regulation. The platform becomes a reflection of your business's commitment to not just surviving, but thriving within the American dream.

Customizing Your Settings

Tailoring QuickBooks for the U.S. Market: Taxes, Language, and Currency

In the mosaic that is U.S. commerce, where every chip of colored glass tells a story of cultural and economic diversity, QuickBooks stands as a unifying framework, designed to embrace each unique narrative. Tailoring QuickBooks for the diverse American market is akin to fine-tuning a musical instrument before a grand concert of enterprise. Herein lies the art of personalizing a tool to resonate with the melodies of American tax laws, the dialects of commerce, and the pulsing currency that fuels the economy's heartbeat.

When we discuss taxes within QuickBooks, we are not merely inputting numbers but are navigating the labyrinth of U.S. tax regulations—a task akin to cartography, where each state's sales tax is a new territory to be charted. The QuickBooks wizard is the cartographer's compass, guiding business owners through the complex terrain of tax rates that vary from the sun-kissed beaches of California to the bustling streets of New York. This is a journey through a fiscal landscape where not just sales tax, but also use tax, excise tax, and others, demand recognition and respect.

Taxes in the U.S. are more than just statutory obligations; they are a tapestry woven with countless threads, each a statute or ordinance. QuickBooks becomes the loom on which this tapestry is delicately crafted. Setting up the correct tax agency pays homage to the pillars of federal and state revenue systems, ensuring that every transaction acknowledges its dues to the grand treasury of civilization.

As for language, QuickBooks transcends the Tower of Babel that is America's linguistic plurality. In its ledger lines and report summaries, it speaks a universal tongue, yet it is sensitive to the nuances that cater to the local dialects of commerce. This is not just about choosing 'English (U.S.)' from a dropdown menu; it's about aligning the software's lexicon to the vernacular of American trade, where terms like 'check' and 'inventory' carry the weight of daily business interactions.

Currency, the lifeblood of any economic body, takes on a heightened importance in QuickBooks' setup for U.S. businesses. The dollar, with its iconic visage of past presidents, is not simply a unit of measurement in QuickBooks. It is the standard by which all financial achievements are gauged, the yardstick of success. Here, the software's currency settings are not static figures but dynamic embodiments of the market's pulse, flexing with the ebb and flow of exchange rates and economic tides.

Within the digital halls of QuickBooks, currency conversion is a quiet sentinel, ever vigilant, ensuring that each international transaction is converted into the familiar cadence of dollars and cents. It is here that QuickBooks exhibits its prowess as a tool for the American entrepreneur who ventures beyond domestic borders, ensuring their financial narrative remains uninterrupted by the babel of global currencies.

For the American business owner, customizing QuickBooks' settings for taxes, language, and currency is an initiation ritual. It is an intimate dance with the nuances of national and state guidelines, a choreography that aligns with the symphony of market demands. Through this process, QuickBooks becomes more than a ledger-keeping machine; it transforms into a beacon of compliance, a linguistic bridge, and a monetary translator that guides the U.S. entrepreneur through the Gordian knot of conducting business in the land of opportunity.

Industry-Specific Settings: Best Practices for U.S. Microbusinesses

The economic landscape of the United States is dotted with a constellation of microbusinesses, each with its own set of unique demands and challenges. QuickBooks has positioned itself as a versatile chameleon, tailoring its features to meet the nuanced needs of these small yet mighty enterprises. The success of a microbusiness hinges not just on the quality of its products or services but also on the meticulous management of its financial backbone. Here, QuickBooks serves as a pivotal resource, offering industry-specific settings that cater to the diverse tapestry of American entrepreneurship.

In the vibrant world of retail, QuickBooks demonstrates its prowess in inventory management. A clothing boutique in downtown San Francisco, for instance, can utilize QuickBooks to monitor its trendy apparel lines, automatically updating stock levels with each sale and return. This real-time inventory tracking transcends mere numbers; it tells the story of consumer trends, seasonal demands, and the ebb and flow of fashion waves. QuickBooks empowers retailers to not only manage their inventory with precision but also to glean insights that drive purchasing decisions, sales strategies, and ultimately, business growth.

When we pivot to the bustling kitchens of cafes and bistros, QuickBooks artfully blends the creative with the analytical. For a family-run patisserie in New Orleans, QuickBooks becomes an extension of the kitchen itself, managing ingredient inventories while keeping an eye on the bottom line. The software's adaptability allows for menu item cost analysis, which aids in pricing decisions that respect both the craft of baking and the necessity of profit. In this way, QuickBooks helps culinary entrepreneurs marry their passion for food with financial wisdom.

Service-based microenterprises, from digital marketing agencies in New York to plumbing services in rural Nebraska, find in QuickBooks a responsive ally. QuickBooks facilitates the tailoring of service items and invoicing templates to reflect the unique offerings of each enterprise. A freelance graphic designer, for instance, can utilize QuickBooks to track project time, billable hours, and expenses, turning the abstracts of creativity into concrete figures that reflect the value of their art.

The robustness of QuickBooks truly shines through in the hands of contractors and tradespeople. For a small construction firm in Texas, QuickBooks offers a sturdy framework for job costing and expense tracking. It allows builders to see the financial landscape of their projects with clarity, ensuring that every nail, tile, and hour of labor is accounted for. This meticulous financial tracking enables builders to place accurate bids, manage budgets effectively, and carve out a competitive edge in the construction market.

Non-profits, bound by their mission-driven nature and the scrutiny that comes with handling public funds, find in QuickBooks a financial steward of unmatched diligence. A charitable organization in Chicago can leverage QuickBooks to track donations, manage grants, and produce detailed reports that stand up to the examination of boards, donors, and regulators. QuickBooks does more than record transactions for non-profits; it reinforces trust through transparency and accountability.

The customization does not end with setting selection; it extends to the integration of QuickBooks with other specialized tools. A tech startup in Silicon Valley, for example, may integrate QuickBooks with a CRM system to synchronize financial data with customer interactions, creating a cohesive view of the business's health.

To distill best practices from QuickBooks' extensive offerings, microbusiness owners must engage in a thoughtful selection process, identifying the tools and features that resonate most closely with their industry's specific rhythm. It may be tempting to activate every available feature, but the artistry lies in curating an experience that aligns with the business's unique tempo. This careful customization transforms QuickBooks from a generic accounting platform into a finely-tuned instrument that plays in concert with the business's operations.

Ultimately, QuickBooks is more than a software solution; it's a catalyst for microbusiness success. By offering a deep bench of industry-specific settings, QuickBooks not only speaks the language of each sector but also anticipates its needs, evolves with its growth, and, most importantly, champions its journey toward financial acuity and success.

In the final strokes of setting up your QuickBooks account, the meticulous craftsmanship of customization comes to fruition. You've navigated through the essential steps, tailored each setting to the precise demands of your industry, and poised your business for operational excellence. QuickBooks now stands as a testament to your commitment to financial clarity and control, equipped to handle the ebbs and flows of the American business tide. With your digital ledger crafted to the contours of your company's needs, you embark forward, empowered with the tools to capture the full spectrum of your business's financial narrative. As your enterprise unfolds, QuickBooks will continue to adapt, providing a steadfast platform for your ongoing journey through the American economic landscape.

Chapter 3: Navigating the Dashboard

Navigating the QuickBooks dashboard is akin to embarking on a voyage through the financial narrative of your business. It's where numbers transform into insights, and clicks into commands that propel your enterprise forward. This journey through QuickBooks offers a dynamic interaction with every aspect of your financial story, fostering a connection that transcends the conventional. As we unpack the essence of the dashboard, we uncover a world where each icon is a gateway and every shortcut, a path to operational excellence. It's a realm where efficiency meets intuition, guiding you through a seamless fusion of data and action, tailored for the astute American entrepreneur.

Key Features and Icons

Dashboard Essentials for U.S. Users: What You Need to Know

Navigating the digital corridors of QuickBooks' dashboard is akin to mastering the helm of your business's financial ship. It's where insights bloom like night-blooming jasmine, subtly revealing the financial health of your enterprise with each refresh. This dashboard, your command center, embodies a fusion of simplicity and complexity, designed to cater to both the uninitiated and the financially astute business owner.

Upon logging into QuickBooks, U.S. users are greeted with a panoramic view of their economic landscape. Here, the dashboard offers a symphony of widgets and modules, each narrating a different fiscal tale. Sales figures dance across the screen, illustrating peaks and troughs in a visual sonnet. Beneath them, expense summaries paint a stark, honest picture of outflows, as necessary as they are instructive.

For the American entrepreneur, this dashboard becomes a window into the ebb and flow of business tides. The 'Bank Accounts' widget consolidates your financial reservoirs, providing a real-time glance at cash flows, akin to a fiscal heartbeat. Meanwhile, 'Invoices' and 'Expenses' serve as the diligent librarians of your financial records, tracking every dollar with an almost archival precision.

But the dashboard's true magic lies in its customization – a canvas for the user to curate their financial narrative. It's not merely about displaying data; it's about telling the user's unique business story through numbers and charts. Whether you wish to prioritize accounts receivable to keep a pulse on incoming funds or focus on expense reports to scrutinize cash outflow, the dashboard bends to the will of your business priorities.

The 'Profit and Loss' widget stands as a sentinel, a testament to the health of your enterprise. Here, the visceral reality of your business acumen is laid bare – profits are not just numbers, but the lifeblood of your business, signaling growth and stability or warning of challenges ahead. It is this widget that often draws the focused gaze of the discerning business owner, interpreting the silent language of rise and fall in the context of their business dreams.

Further down, the 'Sales Tax' module is a constant reminder of the civic dance every business must partake in. It demystifies the oft-complex tax implications for the layperson, presenting tax data with clarity and timeliness. This serves as a beacon for compliance, ensuring that the business not only thrives in the present but also secures its standing in the landscape of governmental obligations.

The QuickBooks dashboard does not merely inform; it educates. It engages the user in an ongoing dialogue about their business's financial narrative. With each login, the entrepreneur is schooled in the delicate art of balance, learning to weigh revenue against expense, growth against stability. It is a tool that has evolved to speak the language of intuition, not just numbers.

Navigating this dashboard is a journey that begins with the foundational knowledge of what each widget represents, but it blossoms into a strategic dance of financial decision-making. As the business grows, the dashboard grows with it, introducing new widgets and data points that mirror the expanding complexities of a thriving enterprise.

In the narrative of American small businesses, where agility and informed decision-making are pivotal, the QuickBooks dashboard is more than a tool; it's a steadfast ally. It assures that even on days when the waters of commerce are choppy, the captain of the ship has a clear view of the horizon and the charts to navigate forward.

In the tapestry of the dashboard's offerings, even the minutiae matter—the subtle alerts and reminders that nudge the business owner towards actions and deadlines. The 'Tasks' feature is the silent sentinel, ensuring nothing slips through the cracks in the entrepreneurial journey. It's here where the mingling of operational duties with financial oversight takes place, serving as the crucible where efficiency is forged.

American entrepreneurs have a penchant for agility, a trait reflected in the 'Recent Transactions' widget. It's like having a financial journal that never sleeps, constantly updated, providing a scroll of the most recent fiscal actions—a ledger for the digital age. It reinforces the power of real-time data, enabling businesses to pivot with precision, reacting to the present with an eye on the future.

For those who seek a more granular understanding of their business, 'Reports' offer a deeper dive into the fiscal waters. It's akin to peering through a financial microscope, revealing the inner workings of the business in vivid detail. Here, custom reports become narratives that can be tailored to answer specific questions about the business's financial journey, offering insights that go beyond the surface.

Yet, it is not all about reflection. The dashboard's 'Goals' feature serves as a beacon for ambition, allowing users to set financial targets and track progress towards them. This is where dreams get quantified, where visions get translated into measurable milestones. The American dream, with its intrinsic pursuit of growth and success, finds a home in this simple, yet profound, aspect of the QuickBooks experience.

Moreover, the integration of the 'Cash Flow' projector is like having a financial oracle at your disposal. It takes the pulse of the present and forecasts the financial future, allowing for strategic adjustments before potential issues become problematic. For the U.S. entrepreneur, whose survival often hinges on the ability to anticipate and adapt, this tool is a cornerstone of financial planning.

But the QuickBooks dashboard isn't just about the individual; it acknowledges the collective efforts that drive a business. The 'My Accountant' widget provides a bridge between the business owner and their financial advisor. It's a collaborative space where financial dialogue can flourish, ensuring that the expertise of an accountant is just a click away, fostering a partnership that bolsters the business's financial acumen.

To navigate the QuickBooks dashboard is to engage with an ecosystem of financial intelligence. It is to accept an invitation to a world where data becomes a narrative, where numbers transform into insights, and where the pulse of a business is constantly monitored, analyzed, and refined. It is here, within the confines of this digital domain, that the U.S. business owner finds the power to not just survive, but thrive.

So, the QuickBooks dashboard for the U.S. user is a testament to how technology can enhance our understanding of business. It reflects a commitment to accessibility, clarity, and foresight—principles that resonate deeply with the entrepreneurial spirit. It is not just a feature of software; it is a companion on the journey to success, a journey that is as challenging as it is rewarding.

Feature Focus: Top Tools for American Small Businesses

Nestled within the heart of QuickBooks, there lies a suite of tools each American small business should become intimate with—a gamut of utilities that don't just perform tasks, but empower owners with insights that crystalize their entrepreneurial visions into reality.

Let us unfurl the canvas and detail the gems that QuickBooks has meticulously crafted for the American small business owner. The landscape of tools at the user's disposal is vast, yet each component harmoniously integrates to create a symphony of financial order.

Invoicing emerges as a vital artery of any business, pulsating with the rhythm of cash flow. QuickBooks bestows upon its users a sublime invoicing tool that merges ease with functionality. Crafting an invoice on this platform is akin to painting with numbers—each line item a stroke of revenue potential, each discount a strategic shading. Beyond the creation, this tool also allows the small business to track the lifecycle of an invoice, creating a narrative from issuance to settlement, ensuring that the lifeblood of the business—cash flow—remains vibrant.

Inventory management, a task often laden with complexity, is distilled into elegance within QuickBooks. The integration of inventory tools allows for a clarity of vision into the stock at hand. It is a diligent overseer, alerting the user to reorder points and tracking inventory trends over time. These insights enable the small business to navigate the fine line between surplus and deficit, a balancing act of critical significance in the small business tableau.

Payroll processing, a labyrinthine journey of calculations and regulations, is demystified within QuickBooks. This tool is a stalwart ally to the small business owner, ensuring employees are compensated with precision and punctuality—a testament to the business's respect for its workforce. It isn't just about disbursing funds; it's a conduit for maintaining morale and ensuring compliance with the intricate tapestry of American labor laws.

Expense tracking within QuickBooks is a beacon of accountability, a window into where the financial winds are blowing. It provides the business owner with a magnified view of outflows, categorizing them with such granularity that it becomes possible to discern financial patterns, identify cost-saving opportunities, and make judicious decisions that shore up the business's financial foundations.

The budgeting tool within QuickBooks is a compass for financial navigation, allowing businesses to set fiscal boundaries and chart a course towards sustainability and growth. This tool does more than track adherence to financial constraints; it empowers the small business owner to forecast, adjust, and envision a fiscal strategy that aligns with their overarching ambitions.

In the realm of payment processing, QuickBooks presents a gateway for monetary transactions that is both secure and expansive. Accepting payments becomes a frictionless experience, accommodating a variety of payment methods to ease the customer's path to purchase. For the small business, this tool is a silent auctioneer, ensuring that the barriers between service and compensation are minimal.

The project management features of QuickBooks transcend the typical bounds of financial software, offering a panoramic view of project financials. It enables the small business to tether every dollar to a task, a job, or a project, imbibing each with a clear economic narrative. This vision into project-specific financials allows for an agile management style, reflective of the dynamism inherent in American small business culture.

Lastly, the time tracking tool extends QuickBooks' domain into the realm of efficiency maximization. It ensures that every hour is accounted for, every billable moment captured, and every non-billable second evaluated. This is not merely about tracking time; it's about valuing it, about understanding its direct correlation with the health of the business.

In essence, the tools QuickBooks furnishes for the American small business are not just levers of operation but instruments of strategic vision. They are the silent partners to the small business owner, allies in the relentless pursuit of prosperity. It is through the masterful use of these tools that a small business can sculpt its path in the bustling markets of America, standing as a testament to the ingenuity and indefatigable spirit that fuels the nation's economy.

Quick Tour with Screenshots

Visual Guide: A Snapshot View of QuickBooks for the U.S. Market

Peering into the heart of QuickBooks, we encounter a dashboard that is the epitome of sophistication, a visual storytelling medium that speaks the language of numbers with striking clarity. It is here, within this snapshot view, that the narrative of a business unfolds, frame by frame, revealing the vitality of its financial heartbeat to those who tend to its growth.

As one embarks on this visual journey, the dashboard reveals itself to be a canvas where financial data is not merely displayed but celebrated in its ability to inform and enlighten. It stands as a testament to clarity, with each element meticulously placed to reflect the immediate status of a business's financial health.

Imagine, if you will, a chart depicting the inflow and outflow of resources, a barometer of fiscal activity. Here, QuickBooks offers a graphical representation that is as intuitive as it is informative. This visual tool is a lighthouse, guiding the American business owner through the fog of daily transactions to the shores of fiscal understanding.

The snapshot view in QuickBooks goes beyond static imagery; it captures the dynamic nature of a business's finances. A graph that details monthly expenses dances with the ebbs and flows of outlay, allowing the viewer to pinpoint areas of heavy expenditure with a discerning eye. There is a narrative quality to this, where each spike or dip tells a story of decision, circumstance, and consequence.

Equally compelling is the income overview—a skyline of peaks and valleys, each representing a day, a week, a moment in time where the business either soared or steadied itself. This graphical metaphor does not simply chart numbers; it charts ambition, effort, and success. It provides a mirror for the business owner, reflecting the results of their strategies and sweat equity in real-time.

Furthermore, QuickBooks does not relegate the user to the role of a passive observer; it invites interaction. Consider the accounts payable and receivable feature—more than just columns of figures, they serve as a ledger of promises made and kept, of trust between business and client. It's a relational dynamic, captured in hues and contours that can be understood at a glance.

The snapshot view provides a tapestry where every thread is a transaction, every knot a culmination of commerce. The 'Profit and Loss' snapshot, for example, is not just an abstract concept—it is made visceral, palpable, and imminently graspable, distilled into a visualization that captures the essence of a business's fiscal flow.

Moreover, the dashboard's snapshot extends to the forecasting of financial futures. Here, QuickBooks provides a crystal ball, of sorts, where projections are not shrouded in mystery but presented with the clarity of foresight. This anticipatory guidance empowers the business owner to steer their enterprise with prescience, armed with knowledge of potential financial winds and currents.

Beyond the numbers and charts, the snapshot view also offers a portal to deeper functionalities. It acts as a command center, where one click leads to detailed reports, another to transaction histories, each an artery leading to the heart of the business's financial data.

Let us not overlook the customization capabilities that QuickBooks avails. The dashboard is not a fixed vista but a fluid, adaptable view that can be tailored to reflect the priorities and preferences of the business owner. In this way, the snapshot becomes deeply personal—a financial reflection of the owner's focus and foresight.

QuickBooks' snapshot view of the dashboard for the U.S. market is, in essence, a confluence of art and science—a place where data is transmuted into understanding, where the complexities of finance are rendered into a picture of simplicity. It is here, in this fusion of utility and aesthetics, that a business owner can stand back and see the financial landscape of their enterprise—a landscape that QuickBooks renders not just intelligible, but insightful, not just visible, but visionary.

Interactive Elements: Engaging with QuickBooks Through Clicks and Shortcuts

In the digital era, interactivity is the bloodstream of user experience, a vital element that transforms the static into the kinetic. QuickBooks is no less than an alchemist in this regard, transforming the mundane act of financial management into an engaging, almost conversational interaction with one's business narrative.

The dashboard of QuickBooks is a kinetic tapestry, woven with clickable threads that lead not to mere data, but to stories, scenarios, and simulations of business life. It beckons with the simplicity of its design, inviting the user to explore the depths of its functionality with the ease of intuitive clicks and keystrokes.

Let us delve into the QuickBooks dashboard, a realm where every click is a command, and every shortcut a secret pathway to efficiency. Here, the user does not simply input data; they converse with it, command it, and coax insights from it.

One touch on the dashboard opens a dialogue with financial figures that whisper the secrets of cash flow management. Clicking on a seemingly inconspicuous icon unravels a detailed account of expenditures, each entry a brushstroke in the larger picture of financial health.

QuickBooks shortcuts are the silent sentinels that save time. A keystroke here, a shortcut there, and the tapestry of tasks unravels, leading to a sanctuary of saved seconds and minutes. For instance, the tap of a key might transport a user instantly to the report generation page, a functionality that traditionally would demand the navigational patience of a cartographer.

Navigating through QuickBooks with these interactive elements is akin to orchestrating a symphony, where every instrument is a feature, every note a business transaction. The user becomes both conductor and composer, crafting their fiscal symphony with clicks and codes that blend to create harmony in the ledger.

The interactive dashboard is where immediacy meets precision. A business owner can, with a mere click, peek into the future through projections and forecasts, or retrospectively sift through past financial decisions, learning from bygone transactions. It is a time machine at their fingertips, offering lessons from the past and visions of the future.

Shortcuts are the hidden portals to productivity within QuickBooks. They lie in wait, promising swifter passage through the labyrinth of financial records—a blessing to the time-starved entrepreneur. They are the secret handshake between the software and the user, a pact that promises to turn prolix processes into swift actions.

Consider the power of a right-click within the dashboard. A menu blossoms, a cornucopia of contextual actions and features tailored to the data in focus. This is no random miscellany of options, but a curated selection of tools, each promising to turn intention into action with minimal fuss.

QuickBooks' interactivity extends to customization, a feature that does not merely allow the user to shape their dashboard but to shape their reality within the software. The dashboard becomes an extension of the user's will, responsive to the touch, malleable to the click, morphing to reflect the unique contours of their business needs.

This dialogue between user and software transcends the transactional; it becomes a journey of discovery, where hidden features and overlooked functionalities emerge at the behest of the curious clicker. It is a game of hide and seek, where every discovery streamlines the process, and every shortcut uncovered is a victory.

In QuickBooks, the dashboard is not a mere interface; it is an interactive partner in the dance of business management. The user leads, the software follows, and together they waltz through the complexities of financial operations, every click a step, every shortcut a twirl.

Part II: Basic Accounting Concepts

Chapter 4: Accounting 101

Welcome to the foundational world of Accounting 101, where the backbone of business savvy is not just about crunching numbers, but about crafting a financial narrative. This is where QuickBooks steps in, translating the age-old principles of accounting into a digital dialogue that speaks directly to the pulse of American enterprise. As we navigate through the essentials, we decode the language of assets and liabilities, learn the rhythm of debits and credits, and understand how accurate bookkeeping composes the symphony of commercial success. It's a journey that transforms the entrepreneur into a storyteller, with each ledger entry a line in their business's unfolding epic.

Double-Entry System and QuickBooks

In the vast narrative of business, the double-entry accounting system is the fundamental plot device that has been guiding financial stories since the Renaissance. It is the methodological backbone of bookkeeping, a duality that ensures every financial transaction is both a journey and a homecoming. QuickBooks, in its digital prowess, has elegantly translated this age-old system into a language of clicks and algorithms, simplifying centuries of accounting tradition into a user-friendly interface.

Picture a transaction as a tale of two cities: one where resources depart, and the other where they arrive. The double-entry system mandates that each transaction must be recorded in two separate accounts, creating a symphony of balance where debits equal credits, and the accounting equation remains in equilibrium. In this realm, assets dance with liabilities and equity to the rhythm of financial activity, each step meticulously choreographed by QuickBooks.

QuickBooks, acting as the scribe of this binary dance, ensures that for every action there is an equal and opposite reaction. When a business makes a sale, QuickBooks sings a song of revenue, while simultaneously humming the tune of an increase in assets or decrease in liabilities. This harmony is the essence of the double-entry system—a financial yin and yang that maintains the universal balance of a company's books.

The beauty of this system, as rendered by QuickBooks, is not merely in its precision but in its narrative power. It tells a story of a business's financial journey that is complex, yet profoundly coherent. Each debit entry whispers of acquisition and possibility, while each credit entry echoes with the relinquishment and fulfillment of obligations. Together, they tell the complete tale of a business's economic endeavors.

The double-entry system also serves as a guardian against the chaos of errors and financial missteps. It is a sentinel that stands watch over the integrity of a business's financial reports, ensuring that every transaction is validated by its mirrored counterpart. QuickBooks, as the modern custodian of this system, automates these checks and balances, giving the user a fortress of security against the specter of inaccuracy.

For the American entrepreneur, this dualistic approach is not just a method but a map that charts the course of financial stability and insight. It allows them to navigate the often tumultuous waters of business with the confidence that their financial position is sound, their records immaculate. QuickBooks serves as the compass for this journey, providing clear, actionable insights derived from the double-entry system's robust framework.

With each transaction recorded, the double-entry system, as facilitated by QuickBooks, builds a bridge between the past and the future. It allows business owners to look back with understanding and forward with foresight, transforming the raw data of daily commerce into a strategic asset.

In QuickBooks, the double-entry system is not confined to the ledgers of old but is brought to life through dashboards and reports that speak to the user in a visual language of graphs and charts. Here, the duality of accounting is made manifest in a single glance, offering a panoramic view of a business's financial health that is both broad and deep.

So, the double-entry system is the heartbeat of accounting, and QuickBooks is its modern pulse. Together, they create a rhythm that resonates through the entire body of a business, driving the flow of financial lifeblood from one account to another, ensuring vitality and vigor in the ever-evolving story of commerce. Through QuickBooks, the double-entry system continues to be the cornerstone of accounting, proving that even in the digital age, some classics never fade.

Basic Accounting Terms

Accounting, often perceived as the language of business, is a narrative woven with meticulous detail, where each term is a thread contributing to the story of a company's financial health. To converse fluently in this language, one must first become intimate with its lexicon, a collection of terms that are the building blocks of business acumen.

At the heart of this linguistic tapestry is 'Assets.' These are not mere possessions; they are characters in your business saga— each one playing a role in propelling the plot of productivity and success. Assets are the stalwarts, the reliable fixtures in your financial narrative, embodying value in various forms: cash in hand, properties, equipment, and even the subtle intangibles like patents and copyrights.

Liabilities, their narrative counterpart, are the obligations—a business's promises cast into the future, pledges of payments owed to creditors. They are the plot twists of the accounting story, the challenges that must be navigated to reach the climax of financial stability.

Equity, then, is the culmination of the tale—the protagonist's share in the business once the dust of liabilities has settled. It is the true measure of value that ownership bestows, the residue of worth that remains when all debts have been honored.

Revenue sits atop the income statement like a crown, regal and indicative of success. It represents the fruits of the company's labors, the sales and income generated from the daily toil of trade and commerce. Yet, revenue is but a prologue; it sets the stage for the drama of expenses to unfold.

Expenses, the necessary counterpart to revenue, are the cost of doing business. They are the actors on this stage, consuming resources to create the spectacle that is profit. They range from the salaries of the workforce to the rent and utilities, each a necessary expenditure in the grand production of goods and services.

In this financial epic, 'Accounts Receivable' heralds the optimism of credit extended, the anticipation of cash inflows from customers. These are the pledges of payment for goods delivered or services rendered, a testament to the business's market reach.

'Accounts Payable,' in contrast, are the echoes of purchases made on credit, the whisper of cash outflows yet to occur. They are the ledger lines that hold the melody of trade, the notes that must eventually resolve to maintain the harmony of cash flow.

The 'General Ledger' is the chronicle of your company's financial journey, a comprehensive record that captures every transaction, every event that has a monetary impact. It is the compendium of a business's financial history, each page a chapter, each line an entry that contributes to the ongoing saga.

'Debits and Credits,' the twin pillars of accounting, are the push and pull of this narrative. Debits are not just increases in assets or expenses; they are the intake of breath before the plunge into investment. Credits, conversely, do not merely signify an increase in liabilities or revenue; they are the exhale, the release of resources in the expectation of gain.

Understanding these terms is akin to holding a map while navigating the vast ocean of commerce. They are the coordinates that guide the entrepreneur, the stars by which one charts the course of a business's fiscal destiny.

To become proficient in the language of accounting is to gain literacy in the story of economic endeavor. It is to appreciate the delicate interplay of terms that, when combined, paint a portrait of a business's financial standing. The entrepreneur who masters this language is equipped to interpret the nuances of their enterprise, to make decisions with clarity and foresight, and ultimately, to pen their own chapter in the annals of business success.

This foundational lexicon of accounting is the bedrock upon which the edifice of business is built. As we delve deeper into the chapters of Accounting 101, we hold these terms close, for they are the keys to unlocking the mysteries of financial success and the tools with which we will sculpt our business's financial future.

The Importance of Accurate Bookkeeping

In the realm of business, accurate bookkeeping is not merely a discipline; it's the compass that guides the entrepreneurial ship through the tumultuous seas of commerce. It is the silent sentinel that stands guard over the integrity of a company's financial narrative, ensuring that every chapter and verse of the fiscal story is true to fact and reflective of reality.

Imagine, for a moment, bookkeeping as the art of storytelling. Each entry, a sentence; each ledger, a paragraph. Together, they weave the intricate tale of a business's journey through the marketplace. The accuracy of these financial stories is pivotal; a single misrepresented fact can turn an epic odyssey into a cautionary tale.

Accurate bookkeeping serves as the foundation upon which trust is built between a business and its stakeholders. Investors, creditors, and customers alike look upon the financial statements as a mirror of the company's credibility. A distortion in these records is akin to a crack in the mirror, a blemish that can mar the face of the business in the eyes of those who sustain it.

For the American small business owner, accuracy in bookkeeping is the fulcrum upon which financial health balances. It affects how they forecast cash flow, strategize business growth, and comply with the stringent regulations of tax authorities. When the bookkeeping is precise, the business can confidently navigate tax obligations, sidestepping the pitfalls of penalties and audits that loom in the wake of inaccuracies.

In the dance of debits and credits, accuracy is the rhythm that keeps the books in harmony. Should this rhythm falter, the repercussions reverberate beyond the pages of the general ledger, affecting everything from vendor relationships to the delicate morale of employees. Accurate bookkeeping ensures that every player in the business symphony—from suppliers waiting on payments to employees expecting their wages— finds their part in the score correctly noted, their contributions acknowledged.

Moreover, the practice of precise bookkeeping allows for the granular analysis of financial operations. It provides the lens through which the business owner scrutinizes the efficacy of their operations, identifies cost-saving opportunities, and hones in on the most lucrative revenue streams. This clarity of vision is essential in the American market, where competition is fierce and the margin for error is slim.

Beyond the daily grind of commerce, accurate bookkeeping is a beacon that guides strategic decision-making. It illuminates the path towards investment opportunities, reveals the wisdom of potential cutbacks, and informs the timing of market expansion. The narrative of a business's financial health, told through accurate records, becomes a tool of foresight, a strategic ally in the quest for sustainability and success.

In the theater of business, bookkeeping is the stage upon which the drama of success and failure unfolds. It is the director that orchestrates every scene, ensuring that the actors—revenue, expenses, assets, and liabilities—play their roles with precision. Without accuracy in this directorial role, the entire production risks descending into disarray, jeopardizing the longevity of the enterprise.

As this chapter unfolds, we delve into the principles that underpin accurate bookkeeping, and the best practices that ensure its execution is flawless. It is a commitment that demands diligence, attention to detail, and an unwavering dedication to the truth of numbers. For in the end, the accuracy of bookkeeping is not just about maintaining records; it's about honoring the trust placed in the business by every individual who is a part of its story.

As we close the ledger on Accounting 101, we emerge with a newfound respect for the meticulous art that is bookkeeping. QuickBooks has illuminated the path, simplifying the intricate dance of financial elements into a harmonious narrative that any business owner can orchestrate. From the double-entry system to the precision of well-kept books, we now hold the keys to unlocking the potential of our business ventures. Empowered with this knowledge, we step forward, ready to weave our own success stories with the confidence of financial fluency, and the assurance that our business's fiscal tale is grounded in accuracy and insight.

Chapter 5: Understanding Financial Statements

Embarking on the journey of financial comprehension, we embrace the essence of financial statements as the storytellers of a business's economic saga. These documents, each a chapter in its own right, collectively reveal the narrative of fiscal health and strategic direction. The balance sheet, income statement, and cash flow statement together form a triad that resonates with the vibrancy of commerce, each playing its part in illustrating a company's past performance, present condition, and future prospects. Understanding these statements is akin to reading the vital signs of an enterprise, providing a clear picture that informs every business decision with precision and insight.

Analyzing Financial Statements for Business Decisions

In the grand theater of commerce, financial statements are not mere documents but the scripts from which the fortunes of businesses are read and interpreted. To the discerning eyes of an entrepreneur, these statements unravel the mysteries hidden in numbers, revealing the narratives of profit and prudence, of cash flows and capital. The art of analyzing these documents is akin to a maestro conducting a symphony, each note a financial detail, each pause a potential strategy.

The balance sheet, with its stoic columns and rows, stands as a testament to a business's financial equilibrium at a point in time. It is the snapshot that captures the essence of a business's net worth, detailing the equilibrium between what it owns and what it owes. Assets—those resources that power the business engine—are balanced against liabilities and equity, the claims held by outsiders and owners alike. The entrepreneur who masters the balance sheet's equilibrium can position their business to maintain financial stability and attract potential investors, who often seek the assurance of well-structured equity and manageable debt.

Then there is the income statement, a chronicle of operational prowess over a period. It tells a tale of revenue, the lifeblood of the business, and delineates the journey of each dollar as it traverses through the veins of expenses to culminate in the heart of profit. This statement is a dynamic narrative, showcasing the ability of a business to generate wealth and manage its resources effectively. Business owners turn to the income statement to gauge performance, to cut through the noise and glean the harmony of profit margins that sing of success or whisper warnings of inefficiencies.

The cash flow statement is the odyssey of liquidity, a record of the journey cash takes through a business. It is the most unvarnished of financial truths, revealing not just the profits but the actual ebb and flow of cash within the enterprise. This statement is crucial, for it speaks in the language of reality, beyond the accruals and adjustments. It answers a fundamental question: Does the business generate the cash necessary to thrive and grow? Entrepreneurs rely on this document to make informed decisions about managing their cash cycle, investing in growth opportunities, and ensuring operational solvency.

Analyzing these financial statements requires a blend of scrutiny and wisdom. The savvy entrepreneur looks for trends in these documents, seeking the storyline that threads through the periods. They look for the plot twists—the unexpected shifts in expenses or the surges in revenue—and they read between the lines to understand the subplots of financial decision-making that affect the overall story.

Beyond trend analysis, ratio analysis turns the magnifying glass on the financial statements, revealing insights through calculated relationships between different financial statement items. Ratios like liquidity, solvency, and profitability become the lexicon through which the health and potential of a business are communicated.

In practice, the analysis of financial statements becomes the bedrock for strategic decisions. A retailer contemplating a second location turns to the balance sheet to assess their capacity for additional debt. A manufacturer examines the income statement to determine if the profit margins can fund an expansion into a new market. A technology startup reviews the cash flow statement to decide when to seek additional investor funding.

In essence, the analysis of financial statements is not merely a task but a strategic endeavor, a critical component of business intelligence. For American businesses, these documents are the compass by which they navigate the complexities of economic seas, the beacon that guides them towards informed decisions, and ultimately, the map that charts the course to enduring success.

The Balance Sheet

At the core of every financial decision lies the balance sheet, a document that, at its essence, is a reflection of a company's vitality at any given moment. It is within this financial mirror that a business sees the contours of its fiscal face – assets, liabilities, and equity – each aspect a testament to the company's condition and potential.

Assets, the heralds of value, are not merely possessions but promises of future benefits. They are treasures amassed on the balance sheet's left side, declaring the economic resources at a company's command. Current assets, with their liquidity, promise a swift conversion to cash, fueling the immediate needs of the business. Long-term assets, with their enduring worth, stand as pillars that support a company's future.

Liabilities, the yoke of obligations borne by the company, balance against these assets. They articulate not only the debts owed but also the trust placed in the company by creditors and suppliers – a trust that the company will fulfill its commitments. Short-term liabilities whisper of impending payments, while long-term liabilities cast their shadows further into the future, a deferment that speaks of strategic financial planning.

Equity, the residual interest after liabilities have been subtracted from assets, tells the story of ownership's stake in the company. It is the net worth written in the language of capital, retained earnings, and perhaps the colorful history of stocks and dividends. It is the score of the past's investment decisions and the future's profit expectations.

Together, these elements form the triad of a balance sheet that U.S. businesses analyze to inform their strategies. The balance sheet becomes a tableau upon which business owners project their aspirations and measure their progress. It is a document steeped in the past yet firmly rooted in the present, casting its shadow forward into the future.

In analyzing the balance sheet, an entrepreneur engages with each line as if it were a chapter in their business's story. They celebrate the assets, scrutinize the liabilities, and contemplate the equity. The balance sheet becomes a narrative that speaks not only to what the business has achieved but to where it may venture next.

The balance sheet's power lies in its ability to inform decisions of profound significance. For instance, consider a business looking to secure a loan. The balance sheet presents its case, showcasing the liquidity and solvency that assure lenders of the business's creditworthiness. It is a financial résumé, crisp and clear, laying bare the qualifications of the business for new ventures and partnerships.

In the pursuit of expansion or investment, the balance sheet serves as a compass. It guides business owners through the terrain of their financial reality, helping them to navigate the delicate balance between risk and opportunity. A robust balance sheet, brimming with assets and judicious liabilities, emboldens the company to reach for growth, while a weaker one advises caution, signaling the need to shore up reserves.

The essence of the balance sheet in informing business decisions extends beyond the tangible. It delves into the strategy, driving home the importance of maintaining a balance that aligns with the business's goals. The savvy business owner knows that each asset acquired or liability undertaken is a strategic move that reshapes the balance sheet – and with it, the company's future.

In the theater of American commerce, the balance sheet is not a mere financial statement; it is a stage where the drama of a company's economic life unfolds. The wise entrepreneur uses it as both a script and a performance review, a source of intelligence that informs the actions to be taken on the marketplace's grand stage.

The Income Statement

Within the grand narrative of a business's financial history, the income statement emerges as the chronicler, detailing the saga of earnings and expenditures. It's a dynamic manuscript that captures the economic performance of an enterprise over time, revealing the fruits of labor and the cost of ambition.

The income statement, also known as the profit and loss statement, is where revenue takes the stage, setting the scene with the total income generated from sales and services. It's the top line that heralds the business's ability to attract customers and command market space. But this figure is only the opening act, for it is followed by a series of deductions, each a character with its part to play.

Cost of Goods Sold (COGS) enters, a direct foil to revenue. It represents the expenses directly tied to the production of the goods sold or the services rendered. In the theater of the income statement, COGS is the gravity that grounds revenue, reminding us that each sale carries a cost, each service a price to perform.

Gross profit, the narrative's tension, is the result of this interplay. It's a pivotal plot point that signifies the business's core profitability before the operational intricacies come into play. It's the breath held by the entrepreneur, the pause before delving deeper into the operational narrative.

Operating expenses then take the narrative forward, encompassing the costs of running the day-to-day business. These are the supporting cast – the sales efforts, the administrative backbone, the research endeavors – each vital to the storyline, each demanding their share of the budget.

The opus of the income statement is the operating profit, or EBIT (Earnings Before Interest and Taxes). This figure is the culmination of the business's operational efficiency, a measure of its ability to turn a gross profit into an enduring, operational gain. It's the core of the story, where strategy and efficiency are tested, where the management's prowess is proven.

Interest and taxes are the unavoidable turns in our financial tale. Interest expenses recount the cost of borrowing, the price of leveraging others' resources for growth. Taxes, the dues paid to governance, are the final toll on the journey towards net income. These are the deductions that speak to the business's fiscal obligations beyond its walls.

Net income is the climax of the income statement's story. It is the grand reveal, the final measure of what's left when the curtain falls on the fiscal period. This figure is the takeaway, the essence of the company's ability to not just operate but to thrive. It's a measure that speaks volumes to stakeholders and investors alike, a summary of success or a beacon of caution.

For the American entrepreneur, the income statement is more than a financial report. It's a tool for storytelling, where every line item adds depth and contour to the narrative of their business. It's a document that demands not just reading but interpretation, inviting the reader to understand the story behind the figures.

Understanding the income statement is akin to a reader's deep appreciation for literature. It requires recognizing not just the plot but the themes, not just the characters but their development. The keen entrepreneur reads between the lines, gleaning insights about cost control, pricing strategies, and operational efficiencies.

In crafting the tale of a business's financial year, the income statement holds a mirror to the company's efforts, reflecting its achievements and its challenges. It is in this reflection that the business finds the truths needed to chart a course for the future, to adjust, to optimize, and to grow.

The Cash Flow Statement

In the ecosystem of financial documents, the cash flow statement stands as a beacon of operational truth, narrating the story of liquidity that courses through the veins of a business. It is the chronicle of the company's monetary vitality, a testament to its ability to harness the flow of cash, ensuring that every financial decision contributes to a stronger, more vibrant entity.

Unlike its counterparts, the cash flow statement does not deal in the currency of accruals or the abstractions of profit. It speaks the language of hard currency, of the tangible and the temporal, charting the ebb and flow of actual cash as it moves in and out of the business. This document is the map that guides entrepreneurs through the cash landscapes of Operating, Investing, and Financing activities.

Operating activities are the narrative's heartbeat, pulsing with the day-to-day transactions that define the operational essence of the business. Herein lies the tale of cash generated by sales, offset by the outflows that keep the wheels of commerce turning. Every receipt from customers, every payment to suppliers, and every dime spent on daily operations tells a part of the story, revealing the business's ability to sustain itself on its core offerings.

Investing activities offer a glimpse into the business's future, chronicling the outlays of cash for long-term growth. These are the plot twists of our tale, where cash is exchanged for assets that promise to yield benefits for years to come. The purchase of equipment, the investment in technology, or the acquisition of smaller entities – these are the strategic moves that shape the business's destiny, each cash transaction a step towards a envisioned future.

Financing activities narrate the company's financial strategy, the inflows and outflows that sculpt the business's capital structure. They reveal the entrepreneur's prowess in balancing the scales of debt and equity, of leveraging external funds to fuel growth while ensuring the business remains afloat. Every loan procured, every share issued, and every dividend paid is a subplot in the grand story of financial orchestration.

The cash flow statement is, in essence, the director's cut of the business's financial movie. It strips away the veneer of non-cash items and presents the raw footage of fiscal reality – unfiltered, unadjusted, and unmistakably clear. It is here that the profitability promises of the income statement are held against the stark light of cash reality.

To the seasoned entrepreneur, the cash flow statement is a financial compass. It informs decisions such as when to seek external funding, when to tighten the operational belt, and when to invest in expansion. It allows for the anticipation of cash shortfalls and the strategic allocation of resources, ensuring that the business does not merely survive but thrives in the competitive American market.

Cash flow analysis becomes the business owner's strategic advantage, enabling them to see beyond the horizon of the current fiscal period. It allows them to forecast the impact of today's decisions on tomorrow's liquidity, to plan for the unexpected, and to prepare for the inevitable ups and downs that accompany every business journey.

In conclusion, the cash flow statement is more than a financial document; it is a narrative device that tells the true story of a business's financial health. It is a critical tool that, when analyzed with care, provides the insights necessary to navigate the complex waters of business with confidence. In the hands of a knowledgeable entrepreneur, the cash flow statement is not merely informative; it is transformative, turning the potential of raw data into the power of informed decision-making.

As we conclude our exploration of financial statements, we find ourselves equipped with a deeper understanding of the financial dialect. The balance sheet, income statement, and cash flow statement have unfolded before us, revealing the intricate interplay of assets, earnings, and cash movements. With this knowledge, we stand ready to interpret the financial health of any business, to make informed decisions that are rooted in fiscal prudence. The mastery of these documents is a powerful asset in the business arsenal, a beacon that guides through the complexities of financial strategy and a foundation upon which sustainable growth can be built.

Part III: Everyday Transactions

Chapter 6: Invoicing and Payments

Diving into the financial lifeblood of business, we navigate the crucial processes of invoicing and payments, where each transaction is a step in the dance of commerce. This crucial chapter of fiscal management weaves through the creation of invoices that spell out the terms of trade, to the art of receiving payments that sustain the business's pulse. It's a realm where precision meets customer service, where the timing of cash flow is as essential as the quality of the product or service delivered. As we unfold the pages of QuickBooks, we learn to choreograph the delicate steps of managing late payments, ensuring the dance floor of business remains lively and the music of profitability continues to play.

Creating Invoices

In the heart of every business transaction lies the humble invoice, a document that, while simple, carries the profound tales of trade and agreement. In the American market, where every penny counts and every deal is a story, creating an invoice in QuickBooks is akin to painting a picture that's worth a thousand words, and often, much more in dollars.

The act of creating an invoice in QuickBooks is more than just filling out a template; it's an art form. It begins with the selection of a design that reflects your business's ethos—be it the classic austerity preferred by established firms or the vibrant templates chosen by the daring new startups. The layout of an invoice is the first handshake between a business and its client, setting the tone for the relationship that unfolds.

Each line item on the invoice is a character in your business narrative. With precision, QuickBooks allows you to detail the goods sold or services provided, telling the story of each item's journey from conception to the customer's hands. Descriptions are crafted with care, prices are listed with clarity, and every discount or tax is noted with transparency, ensuring the client's understanding and trust.

But creating invoices is not just about listing what has been sold; it's about weaving the subtleties of business agreements into a document that stands as a testament to fairness and expectation. Terms and conditions are scripted like a well-thought-out plot, payment instructions are detailed with the clarity of a narrator's voice, and due dates are highlighted as the pivotal moments upon which business relationships pivot.

QuickBooks transforms this creation into a dialogue with the customer, facilitating the addition of personalized messages or notes that can strengthen the bond with the recipient. It's these nuances that convert a standard invoice into a personalized story of your business's commitment to its clients.

The invoice number itself becomes a significant marker, a unique identifier in the annals of your business history. QuickBooks automates this process, ensuring that each invoice stands alone in the records, a solitary but connected part of the larger financial story. This number will echo in future transactions, in payments received, and in the year-end tales of bookkeeping.

Invoices in QuickBooks are not mere static entities; they are dynamic and interactive. They allow for immediate sending through email, direct connection to payment gateways, and even tracking, which opens a window into the customer's response. This interactivity turns each invoice into a living, breathing chapter of your business saga, with QuickBooks narrating the unfolding events in real-time.

For the American entrepreneur, creating an invoice in QuickBooks is a declaration of professionalism. It's a craft finely honed, where accuracy meets aesthetics, and where functionality meets user experience. It's a place where every detail, from the layout to the final total, is a reflection of your business's dedication to excellence and transparency.

Yet, beyond the aesthetic and the narrative, lies the essence of invoicing - the call to action. An invoice is a siren's song for payment, a gentle reminder of the value exchanged and the value expected in return. It is the final act in the transactional play, where QuickBooks ensures that every element, every number, and every term works in concert to secure the business's lifeblood - cash flow.

So, creating invoices in QuickBooks is a critical business function elevated to an art form. It's the bridge between services rendered and revenues realized, a bridge constructed with the tools of clarity, precision, and professionalism. It's a function that, when done right, can enhance relationships, streamline cash flow, and tell the ongoing story of a business thriving in the competitive American market.

Receiving Payments

The reception of payments in the world of business is akin to the heartbeat of commerce, a rhythmic pulsing that signifies the exchange of value and the vitality of enterprise. In QuickBooks, the process of receiving payments is transformed into a symphony of efficiency and satisfaction, resonating with the cadence of successful transactions.

When a payment lands in the hands of a business owner, it is not just the culmination of a sale; it is the affirmation of a job well done, a service well rendered, or a product well received. QuickBooks treats each payment as a critical note in the fiscal melody, ensuring it is recorded with precision and linked seamlessly to its corresponding invoice. This harmony between invoicing and payment is the dance of credit and debit, a balance that QuickBooks choreographs with elegant automation.

The 'Receive Payment' function in QuickBooks is a portal to liquidity, a digital acknowledgment of financial commitments met. As a payment is recorded, the software deftly matches it to the appropriate invoice, mitigating the chances of errors and discrepancies. This is a narrative where details matter; the date, the amount, the method of payment—each is a verse in the revenue story, each a character in the financial narrative.

For businesses operating in the vigorous American market, the versatility of QuickBooks in handling diverse payment methods is a boon. From the traditional checks to the modern avenues of credit cards and electronic payments, QuickBooks accommodates the full spectrum, reflecting the multifaceted ways in which business is conducted in today's age. It's a reflection of a marketplace where adaptability is key, and customer convenience is paramount.

Moreover, QuickBooks does not just passively record these transactions; it actively manages the deposits. The 'Undeposited Funds' feature acts as a staging area for payments, a financial antechamber where receipts gather before being bundled into bank deposits. This step is crucial for maintaining an organized cash flow and for ensuring that bank records mirror book entries accurately—a reflection of financial prudence.

In the event of partial payments, QuickBooks maintains the story's continuity, tracking the outstanding balance with the diligence of a vigilant custodian. Each partial payment is a subplot in the broader revenue story, a stepping stone towards complete financial resolution. The software allows for meticulous tracking of these payment installments, ensuring that each partial payment is a stitch in the fabric of fiscal integrity.

The 'Sales Receipt' function sings a different tune, one for transactions where payment is received immediately. It's a straightforward financial chorus, echoing the simplicity of point-of-sale transactions, where the exchange of value is immediate, and the need for follow-up is nil.

Payment processing in QuickBooks is also a secure affair, a fortress where sensitive financial information is guarded with layers of encryption and security protocols. In a digital era where data is as precious as currency, QuickBooks stands as a bulwark, defending against the cyber threats that lurk in the shadows of transactions.

So, receiving payments in QuickBooks is a multifaceted process, one that touches the core of a business's financial operations. It's a process that demands accuracy, flexibility, and security—qualities that QuickBooks provides in abundance. For the discerning American entrepreneur, QuickBooks is more than a tool; it is a partner in commerce, an ally in the quest for prosperity, and a custodian of the revenues that fuel the journey of business success.

Managing Late Payments

In the bustling marketplace, late payments are akin to unexpected pauses in a melody, moments where the expected flow of cash encounters a silence that can unsettle the rhythm of business. Managing these moments requires not just financial acumen but a blend of diplomacy and determination, a balance that QuickBooks helps businesses navigate with grace and efficiency.

The narrative of late payments begins with an invoice overdue, a story where anticipated cash has yet to grace the ledgers. In QuickBooks, this chapter opens with gentle reminders, automated alerts that nudge customers with the professionalism of a courteous host, reminding them of their commitments without overstepping the bounds of respect.

These reminders are customizable scripts, composed in the language of the business's culture, reflecting its values and its understanding of the fragile nature of customer relationships. They are dispatches sent out into the world, carrying the hope of resolution and the tact of seasoned diplomacy.

As the days pass, the plot thickens. QuickBooks enables businesses to escalate their communications with tactful precision, increasing the frequency of reminders or changing their tone from a soft chime to a firm, yet polite, clarion call. Throughout this process, QuickBooks records each act, each reminder, and each response, documenting the narrative as it unfolds.

For the entrepreneur, this dance is a delicate one. They must keep step with the cadence of persistence while avoiding the missteps that could strain the customer relationship. It's a performance that demands both consistency and adaptability—traits that QuickBooks embodies with its flexible communication settings and tracking capabilities.

But what of the invoices that echo back only silence? QuickBooks does not leave businesses in the lurch. The software equips them with reports and dashboards that spotlight these outstanding accounts, allowing for a strategic approach to managing late payments. It's a tool that transforms potential cash flow disruptions into opportunities for strategic contact and resolution.

In situations where invoices continue to age without payment, QuickBooks provides the means to delve deeper. The business can analyze customer payment patterns, assess the creditworthiness, and make informed decisions on future sales terms. It's an analytical approach, one that values the data-driven insights QuickBooks offers as a guide through the maze of accounts receivable management.

Moreover, QuickBooks connects businesses with integrated options for financing. Through partnerships with lending platforms, businesses can offset the impact of late payments by factoring receivables, turning potential losses into immediate cash flow, a testament to the software's robust ecosystem.

When all else has been tried, and the accounts still lay dormant, QuickBooks stands ready to assist in the transition of overdue accounts to collections. This final chapter is approached with the gravity it deserves, documenting every step to ensure that the business's actions remain above reproach.

The journey of managing late payments is one that QuickBooks maps with care and precision. It is a path walked by many businesses, where the steps of proactive management, strategic communication, and decisive action are guided by the software's hand. In the arena of American commerce, where cash is king, QuickBooks serves as a trusted advisor, a mediator, and, when necessary, a bridge to resolution.

In the ebb and flow of business transactions, the chapter on invoicing and payments closes with a sense of accomplishment and foresight. We've journeyed through the meticulous crafting of invoices, the satisfaction of receiving payments, and the strategic navigation of late payments, all within the realm of QuickBooks. These pages are more than ledgers and records; they are a testament to a business's health, signaling the beat of its operations and the care in its client relationships. As we turn the final page, we carry with us the knowledge and tools to continue the dance of business with confidence, keeping the rhythm of revenue strong and the harmony of customer trust intact.

Chapter 7: Expenses and Bills

Embarking on the critical journey of managing expenses and bills, this chapter delves into the heart of financial prudence and strategic planning. In the realm of business, mastering the art of recording expenses, paying bills on time, and budgeting effectively is not just a practice but a pivotal aspect of sustainability and growth. Through the lens of QuickBooks, these processes transform from mundane tasks to strategic activities that fuel informed decision-making. As we navigate the nuances of each aspect, from the precise recording of every outlay to the careful allocation of resources, we uncover the rhythm of efficient financial management. This journey equips businesses with the tools to maintain a healthy cash flow, foster strong vendor relationships, and pave the way for financial stability.

Recording Expenses

In the grand tapestry of business management, the meticulous recording of expenses in QuickBooks is akin to the precise brushstrokes of a master painter, each stroke adding depth and dimension to the financial picture of a business. This process, though seemingly routine, is a crucial element in the narrative of business success, as it lays bare the truth of operational costs and financial commitments.

The journey of recording expenses begins with the categorization of each outlay, a critical step that demands both attention and insight. QuickBooks serves as an adept guide through this landscape, offering a palette of expense categories that span the spectrum of business operations. From office supplies to travel costs, from utilities to professional services, each category is a chapter in the story of the business's operational endeavors, a detailed account of its fiscal movements.

This meticulous categorization is not merely a clerical task; it is a strategic endeavor. It allows the business owner to glean insights into spending patterns, to identify areas where costs can be trimmed, and to make informed decisions about resource allocation. In QuickBooks, each recorded expense contributes to a broader understanding of the business's financial health, offering clues to the sustainability and efficiency of its operations.

The act of recording an expense in QuickBooks is a multi-dimensional process. The software not only captures the amount but also the date, the vendor, and the payment method. This detailed capture of information turns each transaction into a data point, a piece of the puzzle that completes the financial picture. It is through this granularity that QuickBooks transforms raw data into actionable business intelligence.

For American businesses, where agility and precision are key to navigating the competitive landscape, the ability to record and analyze expenses efficiently is indispensable. QuickBooks streamlines this process, enabling businesses to swiftly record transactions, either manually or through automated tools like bank feeds and receipt scanning. This ease of recording ensures that no expense slips through the cracks, that every dollar spent is accounted for and analyzed.

The integration of receipt scanning technology in QuickBooks is a testament to the software's commitment to accuracy and convenience. It allows users to capture expense receipts on the go, transforming paper trails into digital records with a click. This feature not only saves time but also ensures that records are complete and audit-ready, a safeguard against the pitfalls of lost or forgotten receipts.

Furthermore, QuickBooks elevates expense recording with its reporting capabilities. The software generates comprehensive reports that offer a window into the business's spending habits. These reports, customizable and insightful, allow business owners to track expenses over time, compare costs across periods, and identify trends that inform budgeting and financial planning.

Yet, the recording of expenses in QuickBooks is more than a functional necessity; it is a strategic tool. It empowers businesses to maintain tight control over cash flow, to forecast future spending, and to plan for financial sustainability. In a landscape where cash flow is the lifeblood of business, QuickBooks ensures that every financial outflow is recorded, analyzed, and understood.

So, recording expenses in QuickBooks is a crucial aspect of business management, one that requires diligence, accuracy, and strategic thinking. It's a process that gives business owners a clear view of where their money is going, allowing them to make informed decisions about their operations and strategies. In the hands of a discerning entrepreneur, QuickBooks becomes more than a software solution; it becomes a partner in financial stewardship, guiding businesses towards fiscal responsibility and long-term success.

Paying Bills

In the intricate dance of business finance, paying bills is a step that cannot be overlooked or underestimated. It's a rhythm that, when executed with precision, maintains the harmony of cash flow and fortifies the trust between a business and its suppliers. In QuickBooks, this essential function is transformed into an orchestrated performance where accuracy meets efficiency.

The act of paying bills in QuickBooks is akin to conducting a symphony of financial obligations. Each payment is a note that must be played at just the right time, with just the right intensity, to maintain the fiscal melody of the business. This process begins with the meticulous organization of bills, a task that QuickBooks handles with deft proficiency.

Within QuickBooks, every bill recorded is not just an entry but a commitment. The software serves as a repository of these commitments, organizing them by due dates, amounts, and vendors. This organization is the first step in a strategic approach to bill payment—a method that not only fulfills obligations but also optimizes cash flow.

The American entrepreneur faces a landscape where timing is as crucial as accuracy. QuickBooks aids in this by providing a clear view of upcoming due dates, ensuring that payments are made in a timely manner to avoid late fees and maintain healthy supplier relationships. This foresight is a tool of strategic planning, allowing businesses to navigate the ebbs and flows of cash availability.

For businesses juggling multiple bills, QuickBooks offers the functionality to prioritize payments. This feature is a lifeline in times of tight cash flow, allowing businesses to triage their financial obligations, paying critical suppliers first to ensure uninterrupted operations. It's a decision-making aid, one that balances urgency with importance, necessity with strategy.

In the realm of bill payments, QuickBooks also stands as a guardian of records. Each payment made is meticulously documented, creating a trail of transactions that speaks volumes during audits and financial reviews. This documentation is the narrative of the business's fiscal responsibility—a story told in dates, amounts, and check numbers.

But QuickBooks goes beyond just paying bills; it ensures that each payment is an informed one. The software's reporting tools provide insights into spending patterns, helping businesses understand where their money is going and identify potential areas for cost savings. These reports are the lens through which businesses can view their financial landscape, making informed decisions that impact the bottom line.

Moreover, QuickBooks offers the convenience of integrated payment options. Whether it's through direct bank transfers, online payments, or traditional checks, the software provides a variety of methods to settle accounts. This flexibility is a nod to the diverse nature of modern business transactions, catering to the preferences and processes of both payers and payees.

In paying bills, QuickBooks also recognizes the need for security. Each transaction is enveloped in layers of security measures, safeguarding sensitive financial information from the prying eyes of cyber threats. In a digital era where data breaches are a constant concern, QuickBooks stands as a bastion of security in financial transactions.

So, paying bills in QuickBooks is an exercise in precision, organization, and strategic foresight. It's a function that demands more than just fulfilling obligations; it requires an understanding of the broader financial implications of each payment. For the savvy business owner, QuickBooks is not just a tool for paying bills; it's a partner in managing them, a system that aids in the delicate balance of maintaining liquidity, nurturing supplier relationships, and safeguarding the financial health of the business.

Budgeting for Expenses

In the vast ocean of business finance, budgeting for expenses stands as the lighthouse guiding enterprises through the fog of economic uncertainties. This critical process is more than mere allocation; it's a strategic maneuver that balances ambition with prudence, dreams with reality. In QuickBooks, budgeting transforms from a daunting task into an empowering journey, enabling businesses to chart a course toward sustainable growth and profitability.

Budgeting in QuickBooks begins with historical data, a treasure trove of past spending patterns and financial outcomes. This historical insight is not just a reflection of what has been but a beacon for what could be. Businesses can analyze previous expenses to forecast future spending, taking into account seasonal fluctuations, market trends, and business growth trajectories.

The art of budgeting in QuickBooks involves categorizing expenses meticulously. Each category, be it rent, utilities, payroll, or marketing, is a chapter in the financial story of the business. These categories are not static; they are dynamic elements that adjust and evolve as the business grows. The power of QuickBooks lies in its ability to provide a granular view of each category, allowing business owners to identify areas where costs can be optimized and resources better allocated.

But budgeting is more than just categorizing; it's about setting targets. In QuickBooks, setting budgetary goals for each category is an exercise in foresight and planning. These targets are not arbitrary numbers; they are informed by market research, business objectives, and financial constraints. They represent a balance between the aspirational and the feasible, between stretching for growth and maintaining financial health.

The integration of budgeting with QuickBooks' broader financial ecosystem is a testament to the software's versatility. Budgets are not isolated figures; they are part of a cohesive financial narrative. Income projections, cash flow forecasts, and profitability analyses all play a role in shaping the budget. This interconnectedness ensures that budgeting is a holistic process, one that aligns with every aspect of the business's financial strategy.

For the American entrepreneur, the agility offered by QuickBooks in budgeting is invaluable. The business landscape is ever-changing, and so too are the financial needs of a business. QuickBooks allows for real-time adjustments to the budget, ensuring that businesses can pivot as needed, whether in response to an unforeseen expense, a shift in market dynamics, or an unexpected opportunity.

Scenario planning in QuickBooks takes budgeting to a strategic level. Businesses can create multiple budget scenarios, exploring the financial implications of different business decisions. This "what if" analysis is a powerful tool, enabling businesses to prepare for various possibilities and make informed decisions.

Moreover, QuickBooks' reporting features bring clarity to the budgeting process. With comprehensive reports, businesses can compare actual spending against budgeted figures, gaining insights into variances and their causes. These reports are not just numbers on a page; they are stories of efficiency, discipline, and sometimes, necessary deviation.

In conclusion, budgeting for expenses in QuickBooks is a critical component of sound financial management. It empowers businesses to take control of their financial destiny, to plan with precision, and to navigate the challenges of the market with confidence. With QuickBooks, budgeting becomes less about restriction and more about strategic financial stewardship, guiding businesses towards their goals of sustainability and success.

Concluding our exploration of expenses and bills, we emerge with a comprehensive understanding of these essential financial processes. Through the capabilities of QuickBooks, the complexities of managing financial outflows are simplified, offering businesses a clear path to fiscal responsibility. The insights gained from recording expenses accurately, paying bills promptly, and budgeting wisely are invaluable. They serve as the cornerstone for maintaining robust financial health, enabling businesses to thrive even in challenging economic landscapes. Armed with these tools and knowledge, businesses are well-equipped to navigate the financial aspects of their operations with confidence, ensuring their longevity and success in the competitive marketplace.

Chapter 8: Bank Reconciliation

Delving into the realm of bank reconciliation, we embark on a meticulous journey of aligning the financial narratives of business records with bank statements. This critical process, facilitated by QuickBooks, stands as the cornerstone of financial integrity and accuracy. It's a meticulous dance of numbers where every transaction tells a part of a larger story, ensuring that a business's financial health is not just perceived, but accurately reflected. This journey is about more than matching figures; it's about understanding the heartbeat of a business's finances, ensuring every pulse is recorded with precision.

What is Bank Reconciliation?

In the complex and ever-evolving narrative of business finance, bank reconciliation in QuickBooks emerges as a crucial chapter, one that intertwines the strands of recorded transactions with the realities of bank statements. This process, often perceived as a meticulous task, is in fact a cornerstone of financial integrity, ensuring that the business's financial records are accurate, consistent, and reflective of its true monetary position.

Bank reconciliation is akin to a detective's work in the financial world, a detailed examination where every transaction is scrutinized, every entry is verified, and every discrepancy is investigated. It is a journey of matching the business's internal financial records against the external records provided by the bank, a task that QuickBooks streamlines with precision and efficiency.

At its core, bank reconciliation is about validation. It's a process that confirms whether the cash leaving an account matches the money spent, and whether the cash entering aligns with the actual receipts. This task, while seemingly straightforward, is a safeguard against errors, omissions, and sometimes, fraudulent activities. It's a process of ensuring that what's recorded in QuickBooks resonates with the story told by the bank statements.

The essence of bank reconciliation in QuickBooks is not merely in balancing figures but in uncovering the truth behind each number. This process often reveals subtle nuances of cash flow – the timing differences between when a check is written and when it is cleared, or the lag between receiving a payment and its deposit in the bank. Each of these instances is a piece of the financial puzzle that bank reconciliation helps to place correctly.

In the American business landscape, where accuracy in financial reporting is not just best practice but a legal necessity, the role of bank reconciliation becomes even more pronounced. It stands as a testament to the business's commitment to fiscal responsibility, showcasing its dedication to maintaining records that reflect its true financial health.

QuickBooks, with its intuitive interface and robust functionality, simplifies the bank reconciliation process. It transforms what was once a labor-intensive task into an efficient, user-friendly experience. Businesses can import their bank statements directly into QuickBooks, allowing the software to automatically match transactions with those already recorded. This automation is a symphony of technology and accuracy, where discrepancies are flagged, unusual transactions are highlighted, and the reconciliation process becomes less of a chore and more of an insightful activity.

Moreover, the process of bank reconciliation in QuickBooks is not a solitary journey but a collaborative one. It involves various stakeholders – accountants, bookkeepers, and business owners – each playing a crucial role in verifying and validating financial information. QuickBooks facilitates this collaboration by providing tools that allow for shared access, review, and approval, ensuring that the reconciliation process is comprehensive and inclusive.

During the reconciliation process, QuickBooks serves as a guide, navigating through the myriad of transactions, identifying those that have been recorded in QuickBooks but not cleared in the bank, and vice versa. This comparison is a critical step, revealing any anomalies that might indicate errors or irregularities. It could be a forgotten transaction, a duplicated entry, or an incorrectly recorded amount – each a clue that leads to greater financial clarity.

So, bank reconciliation in QuickBooks is a vital part of financial management, a procedure that ensures the business's financial narrative is accurate and trustworthy. It's a process that offers peace of mind, knowing that the financial data reflects the real state of affairs, allowing business owners to make informed decisions based on reliable information. In the hands of a savvy entrepreneur, bank reconciliation is not just a routine task; it is a strategic tool, integral to maintaining the financial health and integrity of their business.

Step-by-Step Guide

Bank reconciliation in QuickBooks is a voyage through the financial transactions of a business, a journey that ensures the harmony of internal records with bank statements. This crucial process, while detailed, is streamlined in QuickBooks, transforming it into a navigable and enlightening expedition.

Step 1: Prepare for the Journey – Gathering Your Documents

The first step in bank reconciliation is akin to preparing for a voyage. Ensure you have all the necessary documents at hand – the most recent bank statement, along with your QuickBooks ledger. This preparation is crucial, as it lays the groundwork for an efficient reconciliation process.

Step 2: Opening QuickBooks – Setting the Stage

Begin by navigating to the reconciliation module in QuickBooks. This platform is your command center, where you will reconcile each transaction. Select the account you wish to reconcile, ensuring it matches the bank statement you are working with. This step sets the stage for the detailed work ahead.

Step 3: Entering Your Statement Information

Enter the ending balance and the date from your bank statement into QuickBooks. This information is the beacon that guides your reconciliation process, setting the target for your ledger to match.

Step 4: Matching Transactions – The Heart of Reconciliation

Here lies the essence of reconciliation – matching transactions in QuickBooks with those on your bank statement. For each transaction on your bank statement, find its corresponding entry in QuickBooks. Check off each matched transaction, a process that QuickBooks simplifies with its intuitive interface. This step is meticulous but vital, as it ensures that every dollar in and out is accounted for.

Step 5: Investigating Discrepancies – The Detective Work

If your QuickBooks balance does not match your bank statement, it's time to don your detective hat. Investigate discrepancies by reviewing unmatched transactions. Look for common issues like transposed numbers, forgotten entries, or timing differences. This investigative process is crucial to uncovering the root cause of any imbalance.

Step 6: Making Adjustments – The Path to Accuracy

Once you identify discrepancies, make the necessary adjustments in QuickBooks. This may involve adding missing transactions, correcting errors, or noting any peculiarities from the bank, such as bank fees or interest income that weren't recorded in QuickBooks. Each adjustment brings you closer to the goal of a balanced account.

Step 7: Finalizing the Reconciliation – The Culmination

After making all adjustments and ensuring every transaction aligns, your QuickBooks balance should match your bank statement. Finalize the reconciliation in QuickBooks, a step that effectively closes this chapter of your financial story, leaving you with accurate and trustworthy records.

Step 8: Review and Report – The Reflection

The final step is to review a reconciliation report in QuickBooks. This report is a reflection of your successful reconciliation journey, offering a detailed view of the transactions and adjustments made. It serves as a record of your diligence and accuracy, an essential document for financial review and audits.

Troubleshooting Differences

In the realm of business finance, bank reconciliation in QuickBooks can sometimes resemble a complex puzzle where each piece must precisely fit. Troubleshooting differences is an art and science, combining meticulous analysis with detective-like inquiry. This process, vital for maintaining the integrity of financial records, requires a nuanced approach to unravel discrepancies between a company's records and bank statements.

The first step in this financial investigation often begins with a discrepancy alert during reconciliation. This discrepancy, however small, signals a divergence between the ledger and the bank's account. The task then becomes to trace this difference to its source. It could be a mere timing issue, where transactions recorded in QuickBooks haven't yet cleared the bank, or it might be something more complex, such as an overlooked or duplicate transaction.

Understanding the nature of transactions is key. For instance, checks issued but not yet cashed can create discrepancies. QuickBooks offers a clear view of such pending transactions, providing insight into potential timing issues. It's essential to recognize that some discrepancies are mere reflections of the lag between real-world transactions and their reflection in the banking system.

Sometimes, the issue may stem from incorrectly recorded transactions. An amount entered incorrectly, a transaction assigned to the wrong account, or an entirely missed entry can cause significant variances. QuickBooks allows for a thorough examination of transaction histories, enabling users to identify and rectify such errors. Adjusting these entries often requires a keen eye for detail and an understanding of how transactions impact overall financial status.

In addition to these common issues, bank charges or interest income not recorded in QuickBooks can cause mismatches. Regular scrutiny of bank statements for such transactions is essential. Fortunately, QuickBooks facilitates this by allowing users to add unrecorded charges or income promptly, ensuring that the books align with the bank records.

Another critical aspect of troubleshooting in QuickBooks is the review of past reconciliations. Sometimes, unresolved discrepancies from previous periods can cascade into current reconciliations. QuickBooks' ability to track and report on past reconciliation data is invaluable in such cases, offering a historical lens through which ongoing discrepancies can be viewed and understood.

For more persistent or complex discrepancies, the Reconciliation Discrepancy Report in QuickBooks becomes an indispensable tool. This report provides a detailed account of changes made to previously reconciled transactions. Such insights can be pivotal in pinpointing the root cause of a discrepancy, be it an altered transaction, a deleted entry, or an adjusted balance.

Despite these robust tools and processes, there are occasions when external assistance becomes necessary. In situations where discrepancies remain elusive or the reconciliation issues are too complex, consulting with a QuickBooks expert or a professional accountant is prudent. Their expertise can provide clarity, ensure compliance, and maintain the accuracy of financial records.

Conclusively, troubleshooting differences in bank reconciliation within QuickBooks is a fundamental aspect of maintaining accurate financial records. It requires a balance of systematic analysis, understanding of accounting principles, and effective use of QuickBooks features. Successfully navigating this process reinforces the reliability of financial reporting, ensuring that the business's financial narrative is both accurate and trustworthy. In the dynamic landscape of business finance, mastering this aspect of QuickBooks is not just beneficial; it's imperative for the financial well-being and credibility of any business.

Part IV: Advanced Features

Chapter 9: Inventory Management

Navigating the complexities of inventory management is a critical endeavor in the business world, a balancing act that QuickBooks transforms into an insightful and manageable journey. The art of maintaining the perfect inventory level - enough to meet demand but not so much as to incur unnecessary costs - is akin to a well-orchestrated ballet. In this exploration, we delve into the intricacies of tracking inventory, valuing stock accurately, and implementing loss prevention strategies. These processes are vital cogs in the machinery of a successful business, ensuring that resources are utilized efficiently and profitably. As we move through each aspect, QuickBooks emerges as a vital ally, offering tools and insights that turn the challenge of inventory management into an opportunity for growth and optimization.

Tracking Inventory

Tracking inventory in QuickBooks is akin to conducting a grand orchestra, where each instrument – or in this case, each product – plays a vital role in the symphony of your business operations. This process, far more than a simple tally of goods, is a dynamic dance of numbers, a crucial strategy in balancing the delicate scales of supply and demand.

From the moment an item is added to your inventory in QuickBooks, it embarks on a meticulously choreographed journey. Each product is entered with detailed precision, recording its individual characteristics such as cost, sale price, and associated vendor. This initial step is like setting the stage for a performance, ensuring every actor knows their part and every prop is in place.

As your business operates, QuickBooks becomes the stage where the real-time drama of inventory unfolds. Each sale recorded is a movement in this ballet, decreasing stock levels, while every purchase order received is a step that replenishes and reinvigorates. This constant flow of incoming and outgoing stock is seamlessly tracked, offering you a live, transparent view of your inventory landscape.

In the intricate ballet of inventory management, categorization plays the role of choreographer. By organizing items into various categories – perhaps by product line, seasonality, or supplier – you gain deeper insights into the performance of different segments of your inventory. This organization isn't just for clarity; it's a strategic tool that helps in forecasting, planning, and ultimately in making informed purchasing decisions.

Vendor management in QuickBooks is akin to a partnership in a dance. Each supplier is a partner in your business's rhythm, and managing these relationships effectively is crucial. QuickBooks provides the framework to track interactions with your vendors, from purchase orders to payment terms, ensuring that this partnership stays in harmony with your business needs.

The role of inventory reports in QuickBooks can be likened to a critical audience review. These reports offer a panoramic view of your inventory's performance – highlighting the fast movers that deserve an encore, and the slow movers that might need to exit the stage. These insights are crucial for fine-tuning your inventory strategy, ensuring that your stock levels are not just a reflection of your business's past, but a blueprint for its future.

QuickBooks also shines in its ability to integrate with a suite of other applications and tools. These integrations extend the capabilities of QuickBooks, bringing in advanced features like barcode scanning and detailed inventory forecasting. This extended functionality enhances your ability to manage inventory efficiently, ensuring that your business can adapt to changes in demand and supply swiftly and effectively.

So, mastering inventory tracking in QuickBooks is essential for maintaining the equilibrium of your business operations. It's a strategy that goes beyond mere record-keeping; it's about having the right product, in the right quantity, at the right time. This process helps in reducing waste, maximizing sales, and ensuring customer satisfaction. With QuickBooks, inventory management becomes less of a daunting challenge and more of an opportunity to streamline your business operations, turning the rhythm of inventory into a harmonious melody that resonates with the success of your business.

Inventory Valuation

Inventory valuation in the business world is akin to appraising a treasure trove; it's a process of ascertaining the worth of your stock, a crucial aspect that directly impacts your financial landscape. In QuickBooks, inventory valuation is not just about assigning numbers to items; it's a strategic endeavor, a blend of precision and insight that reflects the true value of your inventory at any given time.

The Essence of Inventory Valuation

Inventory valuation is the financial art of quantifying what your stock is worth. It's more than a simple calculation; it's a reflection of your business's operational efficiency and market position. In QuickBooks, the valuation process begins with understanding the cost of your inventory – an intricate tapestry woven from purchase costs, storage expenses, and other associated costs. This comprehensive approach ensures that the value assigned to each item in your inventory is as accurate and realistic as possible.

Costing Methods: The Backbone of Valuation

The cornerstone of inventory valuation in QuickBooks is the selection of an appropriate costing method. QuickBooks offers various options, such as First-In, First-Out (FIFO), Average Cost, and others, each with its implications and benefits. The choice of a costing method is not arbitrary; it's a strategic decision that depends on the nature of your inventory, market conditions, and your business goals.

- FIFO, for instance, assumes that the oldest items in your inventory are sold first. This method is particularly useful in times of rising prices, as it results in lower cost of goods sold and higher reported profits.
- The Average Cost method smooths out price fluctuations by averaging the cost of all items. It's a method that's useful for businesses with large quantities of similar items in stock, providing a middle ground in inventory valuation.

QuickBooks and Inventory Valuation

In QuickBooks, the process of inventory valuation is simplified through automation. The software tracks every purchase and sale, adjusting your inventory value with each transaction. This dynamic approach ensures that your inventory valuation is always current, reflecting the latest market and business conditions.

The real power of inventory valuation in QuickBooks lies in its reporting capabilities. Financial statements like the Balance Sheet and the Cost of Goods Sold report rely heavily on accurate inventory valuation. QuickBooks provides detailed reports that help you understand how your inventory valuation affects your overall financial health. These reports are crucial for making informed business decisions, from pricing strategies to financial planning.

Inventory Valuation and Business Insights

Accurate inventory valuation offers a wealth of insights into your business operations. It affects everything from profit margins to tax calculations. In QuickBooks, understanding the value of your inventory can help you identify slow-moving items, optimize stock levels, and improve cash flow management.

Furthermore, inventory valuation in QuickBooks is not just a tool for internal analysis; it's a critical component of financial transparency. Accurate valuation is essential for investors, creditors, and other stakeholders who rely on your financial statements to gauge the health and potential of your business.

Navigating Challenges in Inventory Valuation

Valuing inventory accurately can be challenging, especially when dealing with perishable items, seasonal products, or items with high fluctuation in costs. QuickBooks helps navigate these challenges by providing a flexible platform that can adapt to your specific business needs. Whether it's adjusting valuation methods or updating item costs, QuickBooks ensures that your inventory valuation is a true representation of your stock's worth.

So, inventory valuation in QuickBooks is a critical process that goes beyond mere number crunching. It's a strategic activity that gives you a clear picture of your inventory's financial value, influencing key business decisions and strategies. With QuickBooks, you have a tool that not only helps in accurately valuing your inventory but also transforms this data into actionable business insights, steering your business towards efficiency, profitability, and growth.

Loss Prevention

In the intricate world of inventory management, loss prevention stands as a pivotal chapter, where each action taken is not just a measure of protection but a strategic move towards sustainability. QuickBooks, in this realm, becomes not just a tool but a fortress, guarding the assets that form the bedrock of your business. In an environment where every product, every item has its value and significance, understanding and implementing loss prevention is akin to mastering the art of resilience in business.

Loss prevention in inventory management is a multifaceted endeavor. It extends beyond the physical safeguarding of goods from theft or damage; it encompasses a broad spectrum of actions aimed at preserving the value of your business assets. This process involves meticulous attention to detail, an understanding of the vulnerabilities in your inventory process, and the implementation of strategies designed to mitigate these risks.

The first step in this journey with QuickBooks is understanding the nature and scope of potential losses. Losses in inventory can occur in various forms - from the tangible, such as theft or damage, to the more abstract, like administrative errors or obsolescence. Each type of loss requires a different approach. QuickBooks provides the tools to not only identify these risks but also to track and manage them effectively. The software allows for a detailed categorization and tracking of inventory, enabling you to monitor stock levels, turnover rates, and aging of products.

Implementing effective loss prevention measures in QuickBooks often starts with setting up a robust system of record-keeping. Accurate and timely records are your first line of defense. They provide the data necessary to identify patterns that may indicate problems, such as frequent shortages or discrepancies in stock levels. With QuickBooks, you can maintain detailed records of every inventory transaction, from purchase to sale, thus providing a clear trail that can be audited for discrepancies.

Technology plays a crucial role in modern loss prevention strategies, and QuickBooks integrates seamlessly with various technological tools. Barcode scanning, RFID tags, and other inventory tracking technologies can be used in conjunction with QuickBooks to enhance accuracy and efficiency in inventory management. These technologies not only speed up the process of inventory tracking but also reduce the chances of human error, a common source of inventory loss.

However, technology is only as effective as the people who use it. Therefore, cultivating a culture of accountability and awareness among your staff is paramount. QuickBooks aids in this endeavor by allowing you to assign specific roles and access permissions to different users. This feature ensures that inventory tasks are traceable to individuals, thereby fostering a sense of responsibility and reducing the likelihood of internal theft or negligence.

Regular audits and reconciliation are the cornerstones of effective loss prevention in inventory management. QuickBooks facilitates these processes by allowing for regular comparisons between the physical inventory and the recorded data. These regular checks serve as a deterrent to loss, ensuring that any anomalies are quickly identified and addressed.

In instances where loss occurs, QuickBooks provides a framework for responding effectively. The software's reporting features give you insights into the nature and extent of the loss, helping you to understand the underlying causes and take corrective action. Whether it's tightening internal controls, revising procurement processes, or enhancing security measures, QuickBooks provides the data and tools necessary for an informed response.

In conclusion, loss prevention in inventory management with QuickBooks is an essential practice, one that goes beyond mere safeguarding of assets. It's a comprehensive approach that involves understanding the various facets of potential losses, implementing strategies to mitigate these risks, and using technology and human resources effectively. QuickBooks, in this regard, is more than just inventory management software; it's a partner in ensuring the longevity and prosperity of your business, helping you navigate the challenges of inventory management with confidence and control.

Chapter 10: Payroll Management

In the dynamic sphere of business operations, payroll management stands as a crucial function, intertwining financial accuracy with employee satisfaction. QuickBooks elevates this essential task, transforming it into a streamlined and intuitive process. The journey through payroll management in QuickBooks takes us through the vital stages of setting up payroll, executing the payroll process, and the all-important aspects of compliance and record-keeping. Each stage in this process is not just a procedural necessity but a testament to the business's commitment to operational excellence and legal integrity. As we navigate these crucial aspects, QuickBooks emerges as a vital tool, simplifying complexities and ensuring that every step aligns with both the business's and employees' best interests.

Setting Up Payroll

Setting up payroll in QuickBooks embodies a crucial choreography in the world of business management. This process, essential in any business, large or small, transcends mere calculation of wages; it's a meticulous fusion of compliance, accuracy, and operational efficiency. In the diverse and intricate business landscape of the United States, mastering payroll setup in QuickBooks is not just a necessity but an art form that ensures the heart of your business – your employees – beats strongly and consistently.

The journey of payroll setup in QuickBooks commences with a foundational understanding of your business's specific payroll requirements. This initial stage is critical, entailing a comprehensive gathering of essential information, including employee details, payment schedules, and tax information. It's a meticulous gathering of data where precision is key. Every element, from an employee's personal details to their tax withholding preferences, forms an integral part of your payroll structure.

QuickBooks offers a spectrum of payroll services, each tailored to meet varying business needs and complexities. Whether it's the Basic, Enhanced, or Full Service option, choosing the right payroll solution in QuickBooks is akin to selecting the perfect instrument for a musical piece; it must resonate with the size and rhythm of your business. For instance, the Full-Service option in QuickBooks, where experts handle much of the payroll process, is akin to having a maestro conducting the orchestra, ideal for those who prefer to focus more on core business functions.

Central to the payroll setup in QuickBooks is the meticulous process of employee setup. This involves inputting detailed and accurate information about each staff member. The strength of QuickBooks lies in its user-friendly design, ensuring a guided and error-free entry process. From basic personal information to complex wage structures, every piece of data adds to the robustness of your payroll system.

Navigating the intricate maze of tax compliance is a critical aspect of payroll management, especially considering the multifaceted tax environment of the United States. QuickBooks serves as an invaluable tool in this regard, aiding in the setup of federal, state, and local taxes specific to your business. Its capability to stay updated with the latest tax laws and regulations is a significant asset, reducing the burden of monitoring ever-changing tax legislations.

Establishing payroll schedules and policies is another vital component of the setup process. QuickBooks' adaptability allows you to tailor your payroll schedule – be it weekly, bi-weekly, or monthly – to align perfectly with your business's operational rhythm and cash flow requirements.

The true elegance of QuickBooks lies in its seamless integration with the broader accounting ecosystem. This integration ensures that payroll data flawlessly syncs with your accounting records, encapsulating every transaction and payout accurately in your financial books. This harmony between payroll and accounting is essential for a transparent and true representation of your business's financial health.

So, setting up payroll in QuickBooks is a blend of strategic planning, compliance with regulatory standards, and operational efficiency. It's a process that ensures not only the timely and accurate remuneration of your workforce but also aligns with legal requirements and integrates with your overall financial system. Mastering this aspect of QuickBooks empowers you to manage a critical segment of your business with confidence, facilitating a focus on growth and success in the competitive and diverse American market.

Running Payroll

Running payroll in QuickBooks transcends the mere calculation of wages; it is akin to conducting an intricate symphony where each note resonates with the commitment to precision, compliance, and employee satisfaction. In the American business landscape, where the margin for error is slender and the demand for punctuality is paramount, mastering the art of payroll management in QuickBooks emerges as a cornerstone of operational excellence.

The process starts with an acute attention to detail, akin to tuning instruments before a grand performance. Ensuring that every piece of employee data is up-to-date and accurate is paramount. This stage involves a meticulous review of employee details, hours worked, and any recent changes in payroll, such as salary adjustments or benefit modifications. It's a critical phase where the groundwork is laid for the entire payroll process.

Transitioning to the calculation phase, QuickBooks becomes a powerful ally, seamlessly integrating various components of an employee's compensation. This includes hourly rates, salaries, overtime, bonuses, and other facets of remuneration. QuickBooks handles these calculations with a precision that mirrors the complexity and nuances of each compensation package. It's a delicate task, where each element must be harmoniously integrated to reflect the true earnings owed to each employee.

But payroll management is not just about the earnings; it's also about the deductions and contributions. This includes accurately calculating and withholding taxes, social security, Medicare, and other deductions, as well as processing contributions to retirement plans and insurance premiums. QuickBooks manages these deductions and contributions with an accuracy that ensures compliance with tax laws and adherence to employee benefit programs. This balancing act is crucial as it not only affects the net pay of the employees but also aligns with legal and financial obligations of the business.

Then comes the crescendo of the payroll process – issuing payments. Whether it's through direct deposit, paper checks, or even electronic payment methods, QuickBooks facilitates a range of options to suit the preferences of both the business and its employees. This phase is the culmination of the payroll process, a tangible testament to the value and appreciation the business holds for its employees.

Beyond the payment, the process extends into meticulous record-keeping and reporting. QuickBooks ensures that every payroll run is accurately reflected in the business's financial records, maintaining the integrity and consistency of financial reporting. This aspect is crucial for maintaining clear financial insights and being prepared for audits, tax filings, and financial analysis.

Running payroll in QuickBooks is not a static chore; it is an ever-evolving process that demands adaptation and learning. As businesses grow and evolve, so do their payroll needs. QuickBooks offers the flexibility and scalability to adapt to these changes, ensuring that the payroll process continually aligns with the business's current state and future aspirations.

In essence, managing payroll in QuickBooks within the dynamic and demanding American business environment is a vital operation. It's an operation that demands not just mathematical precision and legal compliance but also a deep understanding of the human element of business - the employees. Mastering payroll in QuickBooks is therefore not just about managing numbers; it's about orchestrating a critical component of business operations that harmonizes employee satisfaction with operational and financial excellence.

Compliance and Record-Keeping

In the intricate and often daunting landscape of American business, compliance and record-keeping in payroll management are not just tasks to be checked off a list. They are the sinews that bind the financial credibility and legal integrity of a business. QuickBooks, in this context, emerges not merely as a tool but as a guardian of these critical business aspects. It transforms the act of managing payroll from a routine process into a strategic endeavor that upholds the twin pillars of accuracy and adherence to legal standards.

Compliance in payroll is akin to navigating a complex maze of constantly evolving legal requirements. The United States presents a kaleidoscope of federal, state, and local laws, each dictating specific norms from minimum wage rates to overtime, from tax withholdings to employee benefits. The challenge for any business is not just understanding these laws but seamlessly incorporating them into their payroll processes. QuickBooks steps in as a powerful ally here, equipped with features that stay updated with the latest regulations. This ensures that every payroll cycle processed is in line with the current legal standards, thereby mitigating risks of non-compliance.

Moreover, record-keeping in QuickBooks transcends the traditional boundaries of data storage. Each payroll transaction, recorded meticulously, tells a story – of work compensated, benefits provided, taxes deducted, and regulations adhered to. This documentation is the bedrock upon which businesses build their reputation for reliability and trustworthiness. The records maintained in QuickBooks are not mere entries but are narrative threads that, when woven together, present a picture of a business that values accuracy and integrity.

The seamless integration of compliance and record-keeping in QuickBooks is pivotal. When a business processes its payroll through this software, it's automatically aligning its operations with legal standards and creating an immutable record of each transaction. This integration ensures that compliance and accuracy are not afterthoughts but are embedded in the payroll process's core.

The role of QuickBooks in payroll compliance extends to handling complex tax calculations, form preparations, and electronic submissions. This functionality is particularly critical, as it streamlines what would otherwise be a complex and time-consuming process. It ensures that businesses stay on top of their tax obligations, avoiding penalties and fostering a culture of responsibility.

Furthermore, the payroll reports generated by QuickBooks provide invaluable insights. They offer a detailed breakdown of payroll expenses, tax liabilities, and compensations, serving as vital tools for financial analysis and strategic planning. For the discerning business owner, these reports offer much more than retrospective data; they provide a lens through which future business strategies can be formulated and refined.

As we encapsulate our exploration of payroll management in QuickBooks, we emerge with a comprehensive understanding of its pivotal role in business operations. The journey through the intricacies of payroll setup, execution, and adherence to compliance standards underscores the significance of this function in maintaining a business's financial health and ethical standing. QuickBooks serves not just as a facilitator but as a guardian of this process, ensuring accuracy, efficiency, and compliance are seamlessly integrated. This mastery of payroll management is a reflection of a business's dedication to excellence, fostering a culture of trust and reliability. It reinforces the notion that effective payroll management, executed with precision and foresight, is essential for the sustainable growth and success of any business in the competitive American market.

Chapter 11: Tax Compliance and Reporting

Navigating the complex terrain of tax compliance and reporting in the American business landscape is a critical yet intricate task, one that requires precision, adaptability, and strategic foresight. QuickBooks emerges as a crucial tool in this endeavor, simplifying and streamlining the process for businesses of all sizes. This exploration delves into the multifaceted world of sales tax management, federal and state tax compliance, and the art of strategic tax planning. Each element is a vital cog in the machinery of financial management, ensuring that businesses not only adhere to legal requirements but also optimize their fiscal strategies. As we journey through these various aspects, QuickBooks stands as a guiding light, transforming the often daunting task of tax compliance into an opportunity for efficiency and growth.

Sales Tax

Managing sales tax in QuickBooks is a task that mirrors the intricate dance of navigating through a labyrinth of varied and ever-changing regulations. In the United States, where each state, and sometimes each city, has its own set of rules and rates, the challenge of sales tax compliance transforms into a strategic endeavor. For businesses, large or small, this is not just a routine fiscal duty but a critical aspect of financial management, where precision and adaptability are key.

In the American market, the decentralized nature of sales tax regulations presents a unique challenge. Unlike a uniform value-added tax (VAT) system, U.S. sales tax is a mosaic of diverse rates and rules, each jurisdiction with its nuances. This complexity is particularly pronounced for businesses operating across multiple states or those engaged in e-commerce. The initial step in managing sales tax within QuickBooks is recognizing and establishing your nexus – the legal term that defines your obligation to collect and remit sales tax in a particular jurisdiction. The concept of nexus has evolved significantly, especially with the advent of online retail, encompassing criteria such as physical presence, revenue thresholds, or even affiliations.

Setting up sales tax in QuickBooks involves a meticulous process of configuring the software to reflect the specific sales tax rates and rules of each jurisdiction where your business has a nexus. This setup is crucial as it dictates how sales tax is calculated and applied to transactions. QuickBooks offers a level of customization and flexibility that is indispensable for businesses dealing with multiple sales tax rates. It allows for accurate calculation of sales tax, ensuring compliance with each area's specific regulations.

The application and calculation of sales tax in transactions within QuickBooks require a high degree of precision. The software, designed to adapt to the complex nature of U.S. sales tax laws, automatically applies the correct tax rate based on the customer's location and the nature of the product or service being sold. This automation is a boon for businesses, particularly those that operate online and deal with a wide range of customers across different states. It ensures accuracy in tax calculations, thereby minimizing the risk of errors and non-compliance.

Beyond calculation, the process of sales tax reporting and filing is a significant aspect of sales tax management in QuickBooks. Each jurisdiction in the United States may have different filing requirements and schedules, adding layers of complexity to the tax filing process. QuickBooks simplifies this task by consolidating sales tax data into comprehensive reports that provide a clear overview of the taxes collected and owed. This feature is invaluable when it comes to filing accurate tax returns on time, a crucial aspect of maintaining good standing with tax authorities.

In addition to facilitating tax filings, QuickBooks serves as a robust record-keeping system. It maintains detailed records of all transactions, creating an audit trail that is crucial for both internal reviews and external audits. This comprehensive record-keeping is not just a feature of the software; it's a safeguard, ensuring that businesses can confidently verify their compliance with sales tax regulations if ever questioned by tax authorities.

So, managing sales tax in QuickBooks within the complex and varied landscape of American tax law is a critical task that demands more than just a rudimentary understanding of regulations. It requires a strategic approach, leveraging the capabilities of QuickBooks to ensure accuracy, efficiency, and compliance. The ability to navigate the complexities of sales tax laws confidently, adapting to their constant evolution, is crucial for any business seeking to maintain financial integrity and operational efficiency. QuickBooks, in this regard, stands as an indispensable tool, guiding businesses through the intricacies of sales tax compliance and reporting, and ensuring that this essential aspect of financial management is handled with precision and care.

Federal and State Taxes

Navigating the complex world of federal and state taxes in the United States is a task that demands meticulous attention to detail and an in-depth understanding of diverse regulations. For businesses leveraging QuickBooks, this formidable challenge of tax compliance and reporting becomes a manageable, although still intricate, undertaking. Mastering the nuances of federal and state tax laws within QuickBooks is not merely a legal requirement but a strategic necessity for businesses aiming to thrive in the American market.

At the federal level, tax compliance encompasses a range of obligations, from income tax calculations to managing payroll taxes, including Social Security and Medicare contributions. QuickBooks simplifies this intricate process through features that automate much of the tax calculation and reporting. It accurately calculates the taxes to be withheld from each employee's paycheck, ensuring adherence to federal standards. Furthermore, QuickBooks becomes an indispensable tool in preparing for federal tax filings, streamlining the generation of necessary documents like W-2 and 1099 forms, and reducing the risk of errors associated with manual data entry.

However, the challenge amplifies when dealing with state taxes due to the variability in tax laws across states. QuickBooks rises to this challenge by offering tailored solutions for state-specific tax requirements. This adaptability is crucial for businesses operating across multiple states, each with its unique tax regulations. For instance, QuickBooks assists businesses in navigating state income tax requirements and managing state-specific payroll taxes, ensuring that compliance is maintained across all operational jurisdictions.

A particularly demanding aspect of state tax compliance is managing sales tax obligations, especially for e-commerce businesses that sell across state lines. QuickBooks provides essential tools to determine sales tax nexus, automate sales tax calculations, and ensure accurate remittance in accordance with the varying rates and rules of different states. This functionality is vital in a landscape where e-commerce has made sales tax compliance increasingly complex.

Beyond the calculations and filings, strategic tax reporting and planning within QuickBooks play a pivotal role in effective tax management. QuickBooks offers comprehensive reporting features that provide critical insights into tax liabilities, enabling businesses to plan ahead for tax obligations. These reports are instrumental in informed decision-making, aiding in cash flow management and financial planning.

Furthermore, QuickBooks allows for the incorporation of strategic tax planning into the broader scope of financial management. This includes tactics such as income deferral, accelerated deductions, and leveraging tax credits and incentives. QuickBooks enables businesses to model and understand the impact of these strategies on their overall tax liability and financial health, thus turning tax planning into a tool for fiscal optimization.

So, managing federal and state taxes within QuickBooks in the American business environment is a multifaceted endeavor that extends beyond compliance. It involves a strategic approach to handling diverse tax obligations, leveraging QuickBooks' capabilities to ensure accuracy, efficiency, and proactive financial planning. This mastery of tax compliance and reporting is not just about meeting legal requirements; it's about positioning a business for success and stability in a competitive and ever-changing fiscal landscape. QuickBooks, in this regard, emerges as more than just a software solution; it is a strategic partner, guiding businesses through the complexities of tax compliance with precision and foresight.

Strategic Tax Planning

Strategic tax planning in the American business environment, particularly when navigated through QuickBooks, is a sophisticated process that intertwines foresight, meticulous strategy, and an intricate understanding of complex rules. It's an approach that goes beyond merely fulfilling obligations and becomes a proactive form of financial management, significantly influencing the fiscal health and trajectory of a business.

The essence of strategic tax planning is to look beyond the present, analyzing current financial practices to optimize future tax liabilities. This task involves delving deep into the intricacies of tax laws, leveraging every opportunity to minimize tax burdens while adhering to legal frameworks. Within QuickBooks, strategic tax planning is supported by a plethora of data and analytics, providing businesses with the insights necessary to make informed decisions.

Understanding the tax landscape is the first step in strategic tax planning. The United States tax code is complex and constantly evolving, filled with nuances that can significantly impact businesses. QuickBooks assists in deciphering this complexity by offering up-to-date information on tax laws and regulations, a crucial feature for staying ahead of changes that could affect a business's tax strategy.

QuickBooks serves as a powerful ally in identifying tax-saving opportunities. It helps pinpoint deductible expenses that a business might have overlooked, ensuring every eligible expense is accounted for, ranging from office supplies to larger investments like equipment. The software's detailed tracking of income and expenses lays the groundwork for identifying potential deductions, credits, and other tax advantages.

A key strategy in tax planning involves timing income and deductions. QuickBooks allows businesses to defer income or accelerate deductions to a particular tax year based on projected tax rates and financial goals. This could mean delaying invoicing or making advance purchases at the year's end. QuickBooks provides the flexibility and data necessary to make these strategic decisions, aiding businesses in managing their taxable income effectively.

Navigating complex tax credits and deductions is where strategic planning can yield significant savings. QuickBooks assists businesses in identifying and tracking eligibility for various tax credits, from research and development credits to small business healthcare tax credits. Utilizing these credits requires a thorough understanding of eligibility criteria and compliance requirements, areas where QuickBooks offers essential guidance.

Major business decisions like expansions, acquisitions, or investments can have significant tax implications. Strategic tax planning in QuickBooks involves analyzing these decisions from a tax perspective, understanding how they align with the business's overall tax strategy. This might involve modeling different scenarios within QuickBooks to forecast their tax impacts and guide decision-making.

Strategic tax planning is not just about the current year; it's about preparing for future fiscal health. QuickBooks allows businesses to develop long-term tax strategies, taking into account projections for growth, changes in tax laws, and evolving business models. This forward-thinking approach is crucial for sustainable growth and financial stability.

In summarizing our journey through tax compliance and reporting with QuickBooks, we acknowledge the intricacies and challenges that businesses face in this crucial area. The journey has illuminated the importance of meticulous management of sales tax, unwavering adherence to federal and state tax regulations, and the implementation of strategic tax planning. QuickBooks has proven to be an invaluable ally, offering tools and insights that facilitate compliance, reduce risk, and foster strategic financial decision-making. This mastery of tax compliance and reporting is not merely about meeting legal obligations; it's about embedding sound financial practices into the very fabric of a business, ensuring long-term sustainability and success in a competitive marketplace.

Part V: Month-End and Year-End Processes

Chapter 12: Month-End Close Procedures

Navigating the month-end close procedures in the world of business finance is a task of precision and strategic importance, especially in the dynamic and diverse American market. This process, a crucial component of a company's financial management, demands an intricate balance between accuracy and efficiency. For businesses utilizing tools like QuickBooks, this period marks an opportunity to consolidate financial information, assess the company's fiscal health, and prepare for the challenges of the coming month. The journey through month-end close procedures involves a comprehensive checklist, awareness of common pitfalls, and effective strategies to streamline the entire process. Mastering these elements is not just about closing books; it's about weaving a clear and accurate financial narrative that supports informed decision-making and strategic planning.

Checklist and Best Practices

The month-end close process in business finance, especially when navigated with tools like QuickBooks, can be likened to a masterful orchestration where each note contributes to the overall financial health of a company. It's a time when financial data is meticulously consolidated and analyzed, ensuring accuracy and providing insights into the company's fiscal standing. For businesses in the competitive American market, mastering this process is not just a routine task but a strategic imperative to maintain clarity, compliance, and a strong financial foundation.

At the heart of the month-end close lies a comprehensive checklist. This checklist serves as a roadmap, guiding finance teams through the intricate process of reconciling and reviewing various financial elements. Unlike a static list, this checklist is dynamic, tailored to the specific needs of each business. For instance, a small startup's checklist might focus on cash flow and basic expense tracking, while a larger enterprise may delve into complex revenue recognition or international currency reconciliations.

The month-end close begins with the crucial task of cash reconciliation. This step ensures that the cash recorded in the books aligns with the actual cash in hand and bank statements. It's foundational, as discrepancies here could indicate deeper financial issues or clerical errors. Tools like QuickBooks automate much of this process, highlighting mismatches for further investigation.

Next, the focus shifts to accounts receivable and payable. This involves ensuring all transactions within the period have been recorded correctly. In receivables, businesses must review outstanding invoices, flagging any overdue accounts for follow-up. In payables, it's essential to verify all bills have been accounted for and are accurately reflected. This step is critical for maintaining healthy cash flow and sustaining good vendor relationships.

Inventory reconciliation is another vital component, particularly for businesses dealing with physical goods. This process requires verifying that the inventory records match the actual stock levels. Disparities here can point to issues like loss, theft, or administrative mistakes. Accurate inventory tracking, a feature efficiently managed by QuickBooks, is crucial for understanding product movement, cost of goods sold, and overall inventory health.

Fixed assets and depreciation reviews also play a significant role in month-end procedures. This involves recording new asset purchases and ensuring depreciation is accurately calculated. This step is essential for maintaining an accurate picture of the company's assets and understanding their value over time.

The process also includes making necessary adjusting journal entries. These adjustments might include accruals for expenses not yet paid or recognition of prepaid expenses. QuickBooks facilitates these adjustments, ensuring financial statements accurately reflect the company's position at the end of the month.

The culmination of the month-end close process is the generation of financial reports. These reports, like balance sheets, income statements, and cash flow statements, provide a comprehensive overview of the company's financial performance. QuickBooks simplifies this step, offering insights that are crucial for informed decision-making and strategic planning.

So, the checklist and best practices for month-end close procedures are critical to effective financial management. They ensure that a business's financial records are accurate, complete, and compliant. In the ever-evolving American business landscape, mastering these month-end procedures is akin to conducting a financial orchestra, requiring precision, diligence, and strategic use of tools like QuickBooks. This expertise not only solidifies a company's financial standing but also paves the way for informed strategic decisions, driving growth and success in the competitive market.

Common Mistakes to Avoid

In the realm of business finance, navigating the month-end close procedures is a task that bears significant weight, akin to a tightrope walk where precision and balance are paramount. This period, crucial in the financial cycle of any business, especially in the dynamic American market, is fraught with potential pitfalls. Recognizing and avoiding common mistakes in this process, particularly for businesses utilizing tools like QuickBooks, is essential for ensuring the accuracy and reliability of financial reporting.

One of the most prevalent missteps during the month-end close is overlooking the complete reconciliation of all accounts. This lapse can lead to significant inaccuracies in financial statements, affecting everything from cash flow analysis to the integrity of the balance sheet. Reconciliation is not merely a comparison of numbers; it's a thorough review that ensures each transaction is accounted for and correctly classified.

Another frequent error is the incorrect categorization of expenses and income. This mistake can distort a business's understanding of its financial health, affecting profit margins and tax liabilities. It often arises from hurried entries or a misunderstanding of accounting principles. In QuickBooks, automation simplifies this process, but it still necessitates human oversight to ensure transactions are allocated to the correct accounts.

Data entry errors, though seemingly minor, can have a cascading effect on financial accuracy. A single misplaced digit or a transposed number can significantly alter financial results. In the fast-paced business environment, where data entry is often expedited to meet deadlines, these errors can easily occur. QuickBooks offers tools to minimize these mistakes, such as automated data imports and integrations, yet the human element of double-checking entries remains indispensable.

In the month-end close process, overlooking accruals or prepayments can lead to misstated financial statements, impacting everything from business valuation to creditworthiness. The accrual basis of accounting, a standard practice in American businesses, requires income and expenses to be recorded when earned or incurred, not necessarily when cash is exchanged.

Fixed asset management is another area prone to errors. Mistakes in calculating depreciation or failing to update the asset register when assets are disposed of can lead to inaccuracies in the company's asset value. QuickBooks provides tools to effectively manage fixed assets, but it requires diligent monitoring and updating to ensure accuracy.

For businesses operating multiple divisions or subsidiaries, the reconciliation of intercompany transactions is crucial. Failing to properly reconcile these transactions can lead to incorrect financial figures, affecting the overall financial health of the company.

So, the month-end close process is a complex and critical aspect of financial management, where accuracy and diligence are crucial. Avoiding common mistakes is vital for ensuring the integrity and reliability of financial reporting. While tools like QuickBooks offer valuable assistance, they cannot replace the need for a deep understanding of accounting principles and a vigilant approach to financial management. In the competitive American business environment, where financial accuracy is a cornerstone of success, mastering the month-end close process is essential. It not only ensures compliance and accuracy but also provides strategic insights into the business's financial health, guiding decision-making and future planning.

Streamlining Month-End Cycles

Streamlining month-end close cycles in the American business environment is akin to choreographing a complex dance. It's about harmonizing various financial tasks to create a more efficient, timely, and accurate close process. This undertaking, especially for businesses leveraging QuickBooks, involves transforming a traditionally cumbersome and time-consuming task into a streamlined and efficient operation. The aim is to save time and resources, enhance financial clarity, and improve responsiveness without sacrificing the accuracy of financial reporting.

In the pursuit of streamlining month-end processes, technology plays a crucial role. QuickBooks offers a range of features that can significantly aid in this endeavor. Automation is a key benefit here. Automating routine tasks such as data entry, transaction categorization, and aspects of reconciliation in QuickBooks not only speeds up the process but also minimizes human error, a common source of delays and inaccuracies.

A systematic approach is vital in streamlining the month-end close. It involves establishing a consistent routine with clear steps and assigned responsibilities. It's about ensuring that each team member knows their role and has the necessary tools and information. In QuickBooks, this can be facilitated by setting reminders for crucial tasks, using templates for recurring entries, and maintaining a centralized financial information repository.

Continuous improvement is essential. Regularly reviewing the process to identify bottlenecks and inefficiencies can reveal areas for improvement. QuickBooks can analyze task durations and highlight inefficiencies, perhaps suggesting a need to re-evaluate the chart of accounts, refine categorization rules, or reassess workflow to eliminate redundant steps.

Effective communication and collaboration among team members are crucial. QuickBooks provides a platform for sharing data, collaborating on tasks, and communicating efficiently. Ensuring everyone is aligned and working towards the same deadlines is key to minimizing delays.

Empowering the finance team to fully utilize QuickBooks is another critical aspect. Adequate training and resources ensure team members are proficient with the software, leading to more effective use of its features, which results in a faster and more accurate month-end close.

For businesses with complex financial processes, integrating QuickBooks with advanced tools can further streamline month-end procedures. This might include advanced analytics tools for deeper financial insights or add-ons catering to specific industry needs.

The journey through the month-end close procedures culminates in a deepened understanding of its critical role in a company's financial well-being. The process, though complex, is essential for ensuring the accuracy and reliability of financial reporting. In the American business landscape, where financial precision is paramount, a well-orchestrated month-end close process, especially with tools like QuickBooks, becomes a powerful instrument in a company's financial toolkit. It transcends routine bookkeeping, evolving into a strategic exercise that provides valuable insights and sets the stage for future success. This thorough approach to month-end close is fundamental, ensuring businesses are not just financially compliant, but also strategically poised for growth and adaptation in the ever-changing market dynamics.

Chapter 13: Year-End Financial Review

The year-end financial review is a pivotal moment in the business calendar, marking a time of deep reflection and critical evaluation for companies navigating the American market. It's a period where businesses consolidate their financial accomplishments and challenges, setting the foundation for future growth and stability. This review encompasses a comprehensive examination, beginning with thorough preparation for tax season, followed by the meticulous crafting of year-end reports, and culminating in the insightful analysis of financial trends. Each of these steps is integral, providing a clear picture of a company's fiscal health and informing strategic decisions. Utilizing tools like QuickBooks, businesses can transform this complex process into a structured and insightful exercise, ensuring they not only meet compliance requirements but also gain valuable insights for strategic planning.

Preparing for Tax Season

As the calendar year draws to a close, American businesses embark on a critical journey: the year-end financial review. This period is not merely a prelude to tax season but a strategic checkpoint for businesses to recalibrate and reflect on their financial health. For companies using QuickBooks, this process becomes an intricate dance of analysis, preparation, and strategic foresight, essential for navigating the complexities of the fiscal year's end.

Preparing for tax season is a multifaceted endeavor, beginning with the meticulous review of the past year's financial activities. This step involves a thorough examination of financial statements – income statements, balance sheets, and cash flow statements – ensuring they accurately reflect the company's financial status. In QuickBooks, this process is streamlined, allowing for a detailed and efficient review of financial data, ensuring that everything from revenue to expenses is meticulously recorded and categorized.

A critical component of this preparation is reconciliation. Ensuring the alignment of bank statements with the company's records is paramount. This process not only identifies discrepancies, often due to overlooked entries or accounting errors, but also serves as a bedrock for accurate financial reporting. In QuickBooks, reconciliation tools help pinpoint differences, thereby maintaining the integrity of financial records.

Maximizing deductions and tax credits stands as a strategic aspect of preparing for tax season. The year-end review is an opportune time to scrutinize the year's expenses and understand the potential for tax deductions. This could range from operational expenses to capital investments, each offering potential tax savings. QuickBooks aids in this endeavor with its categorization and reporting capabilities, ensuring that no opportunity for tax efficiency is missed.

Compliance and thorough documentation are also crucial. Ensuring adherence to tax laws and organizing necessary documentation, such as receipts, invoices, and payroll records, is vital. QuickBooks facilitates this organization, offering digital storage and easy access to crucial documents, thereby streamlining the compliance process.

Strategic tax planning is an integral part of the year-end review, extending beyond the current fiscal year. This involves assessing future tax implications of current business decisions, whether deferring income, accelerating expenses, or planning significant purchases. QuickBooks can model these scenarios, providing insights into the long-term tax impact of these decisions.

So, the year-end financial review, particularly in the context of preparing for tax season, is a critical process that transcends compliance. It's an encompassing exercise in ensuring accuracy, maximizing tax efficiency, maintaining compliance, and engaging in strategic planning. For businesses using QuickBooks, this period is an opportunity to leverage the software's full capabilities to ensure a comprehensive review of the year's finances. This process is essential in the American business landscape, where fiscal prudence and strategic foresight are key to enduring success. The year-end review sets the stage for a financially sound and strategically oriented new year, allowing businesses to enter the tax season with confidence and clarity.

Year-End Reports

In the annual cycle of business, the year-end financial review holds a place of paramount importance, particularly in the vibrant and competitive landscape of American commerce. At the heart of this crucial exercise lies the preparation of year-end reports, a task that transcends mere compliance to become a strategic keystone in a company's financial health assessment. For businesses employing tools like QuickBooks, these reports provide a detailed, accurate, and invaluable reflection of the year's fiscal narrative.

The year-end reports are not just a collection of numbers and financial statements; they are a comprehensive chronicle of a business's fiscal journey over the past year. Each report, be it the income statement, balance sheet, or cash flow statement, serves as a chapter in this narrative, offering insights into different aspects of the company's financial story. In QuickBooks, the generation of these reports is more than a procedural task; it's an opportunity to gain a deep understanding of the company's financial health.

The income statement stands as a key component of year-end reports, telling the intricate story of a business's profitability. It details revenues and expenses, providing a clear picture of how effectively a business has managed its core operations. QuickBooks, with its precision in financial tracking, ensures that the income statement accurately reflects the company's profitability, highlighting areas of strength and opportunities for improvement.

The balance sheet offers a snapshot of the company's financial standing at the year's end. It is a critical report that outlines assets, liabilities, and equity, and is instrumental in assessing the company's financial stability and liquidity. In QuickBooks, the balance sheet is a dynamic tool that assists businesses in evaluating their financial position and making informed decisions about investments and debt management.

The cash flow statement, an often underappreciated but vital report, sheds light on the company's liquidity movements. Understanding how cash flows in and out of the business is crucial, especially in the cash-driven American business environment. This report helps in evaluating the effectiveness of cash management strategies, and QuickBooks ensures its accuracy and relevance.

Year-end reports serve a strategic role, going beyond a retrospective analysis. They are crucial for benchmarking performance, setting future targets, and adjusting business strategies. QuickBooks allows for deep analysis of these reports, helping businesses identify trends and evaluate the impact of their decisions.

For businesses with specific needs, QuickBooks offers the capability to create custom reports. These reports can be tailored to focus on areas of particular interest or concern, such as departmental performance, customer profitability, or product line success. Custom reports become invaluable for providing insights that inform nuanced business strategies.

So, the preparation of year-end reports as part of the year-end financial review is a critical endeavor, offering businesses a chance to reflect on the financial year and plan strategically for the future. These reports, particularly when generated through QuickBooks, are rich with information that is accurate and insightful. They provide more than just a financial summary; they offer a strategic tool for business growth. In the American business landscape, where financial savvy is key to longevity and success, year-end reports are indispensable, guiding businesses toward informed decision-making and strategic planning.

Analyzing Year-End Financial Trends

As the fiscal year draws to a close for businesses in the bustling American market, the task of analyzing year-end financial trends takes center stage. This analysis is far more than a cursory glance at numbers; it is a deep dive into the financial story of the past year, providing crucial insights for future strategic decision-making. For users of QuickBooks, this process is facilitated by the platform's robust analytics, turning a complex array of data into a coherent narrative of financial health and trends.

The essence of this analysis lies in unraveling the stories behind the numbers. It's about interpreting the financial data to understand not just what happened over the past year but why it happened. Businesses begin by comparing the current year's data against previous years, a practice that reveals trends in revenue, expenses, profitability, and cash flow. This comparative analysis is vital for identifying both positive trajectories and areas requiring attention.

Focusing on revenue trends is akin to checking the pulse of the business. It involves dissecting revenue streams to understand which aspects are driving growth. QuickBooks enables businesses to break down revenue by various categories such as product lines, customer segments, or regions, providing a detailed picture of where the business is thriving and where it is not. This level of detail is critical for pinpointing successful strategies and areas ripe for expansion or improvement.

Analyzing expenses is equally crucial. It's not just about the total spend but understanding how these expenses are distributed across the business. Are there areas of unexpected cost increase? Are there untapped opportunities for cost savings? Through QuickBooks, businesses can conduct a detailed analysis of their expenditures, leading to more efficient resource allocation and cost management.

The crux of this analysis is understanding profitability. Beyond just gross profit margins, it's about dissecting the net profitability to grasp the factors influencing it. This process involves examining costs of goods sold, operational expenses, and any extraordinary items. QuickBooks provides comprehensive tools for this analysis, offering clarity on what factors are impacting the bottom line.

Cash flow trend analysis is crucial, especially for small and medium-sized businesses where liquidity is often a key concern. Understanding how cash has flowed in and out of the business over the year can reveal much about its operational efficiency and financial health. QuickBooks tracks these trends, helping businesses identify periods of tight liquidity and the factors contributing to them.

The culmination of this analysis is in shaping strategic decisions. Armed with the knowledge of past financial trends, businesses can make informed choices about the future. This could involve scaling up successful areas, restructuring underperforming segments, or revising pricing strategies. The insights gained from this analysis are invaluable for navigating the competitive and ever-changing business landscape.

In conclusion, the year-end financial trend analysis is a crucial process for American businesses, offering a window into the financial successes and challenges of the past year and paving the way for informed future strategies. For QuickBooks users, this process is streamlined yet thorough, providing a comprehensive toolset for transforming raw data into actionable business intelligence. This analysis transcends mere number crunching; it is a strategic exercise that informs smarter, more effective business planning, setting the stage for a successful and financially sound new year.

Part VI: Troubleshooting and Tips

Chapter 14: Common QuickBooks Errors and How to Fix Them

In the world of modern business, where QuickBooks is an indispensable financial management tool, encountering and resolving errors is an inevitable part of the journey. This chapter delves into the common errors users might encounter while navigating QuickBooks, offering not just solutions but also insights into the underlying causes. Understanding these errors is crucial for businesses seeking to maintain the integrity and accuracy of their financial data. From network issues disrupting multi-user access to the nuances of banking errors, each challenge presents an opportunity to deepen one's understanding of QuickBooks. The focus here is not only on troubleshooting but also on empowering users with the knowledge to prevent these errors from recurring, thereby enhancing their overall experience with the software.

Error Codes and Solutions

In the intricate landscape of business finance, where QuickBooks stands as a cornerstone tool for many American companies, encountering software errors can be a challenging and sometimes daunting experience. These errors, often manifested as codes, not only disrupt the workflow but also pose a puzzle to be solved. Understanding these error codes and knowing the appropriate solutions is a critical aspect of maintaining the smooth operation of QuickBooks.

One common category of errors in QuickBooks revolves around network issues, particularly when working in a multi-user environment. The H202 error, for example, occurs when a workstation fails to communicate with the server hosting the company file. This error can stem from various issues like network glitches, firewall settings, or DNS settings. Resolving it typically involves ensuring proper network connectivity, configuring firewall and antivirus settings, or using the QuickBooks File Doctor tool to diagnose and fix the network issues.

The 6000 series errors, another frequent occurrence, are generally related to problems with opening a company file. For example, error -6000, -83, often indicates an issue with the company file's location, access permissions, or a damaged company file. Solutions might include storing the company file on a local hard drive, ensuring proper access permissions, or restoring a backup of the company file.

Error 3371 is a hurdle that users may face when activating or reconfiguring the software. It is typically related to issues with QuickBooks' registration and licensing files. Resolving this error often involves deleting the entitlement file, followed by re-registering QuickBooks, which refreshes the software's registration and licensing data.

Banking errors, such as the OL and OLSU series, are commonly encountered during online banking operations. These errors may occur due to issues with the bank's server, data transfer between the bank and QuickBooks, or outdated banking information within QuickBooks. To resolve these, users may need to check for notifications or updates on the bank's website, update their QuickBooks to the latest version, or refresh the connection with the bank.

The 404 error typically signifies connectivity issues between QuickBooks and Intuit servers, often resulting from internet disruptions or server availability issues. Addressing this error involves ensuring a stable internet connection, verifying that QuickBooks has necessary internet access permissions, or waiting for any server-related issues at Intuit's end to be resolved.

So, encountering errors in QuickBooks is not merely about facing obstacles; it is an opportunity to delve deeper into the software's functionality and enhance one's problem-solving skills. Each error code offers a clue, a pathway to understanding and rectifying issues that impede the software's efficiency. In the dynamic and competitive realm of American business, where financial accuracy and efficiency are paramount, being adept at resolving QuickBooks errors is an invaluable skill. It ensures not just the smooth functioning of financial operations but also contributes to the overall resilience and adaptability of a business.

Preventing Errors Before They Happen

In the realm of business finance, where QuickBooks is an integral tool for many American companies, the adage 'prevention is better than cure' holds particularly true. Preventing errors in QuickBooks is not just about avoiding minor inconveniences; it's a strategic approach to ensure continuous, smooth operations and maintain the integrity of financial data. This approach to error prevention, especially crucial in the dynamic American business landscape, serves as a bulwark against the disruption and complications that errors can cause.

A key aspect of preventing errors in QuickBooks lies in cultivating a proactive mindset within the organization. This means regularly updating the team's skills and knowledge about QuickBooks. Regular training sessions and updates on the software's latest features and best practices can significantly reduce the likelihood of user-related errors. When the team is well-versed in the functionalities and potential pitfalls of QuickBooks, the chance of encountering preventable errors diminishes substantially.

Regular software updates and maintenance play a crucial role in error prevention. QuickBooks, evolving continuously, frequently releases updates that enhance functionality and rectify known bugs. Staying current with these updates is essential. These updates not only refine the user experience but also address vulnerabilities that could lead to errors. Regularly updating QuickBooks is a straightforward yet effective strategy to reduce the risk of encountering software-related errors.

Data integrity is fundamental to the smooth operation of QuickBooks. Implementing robust data backup and recovery plans ensures that in the event of an error, the financial data can be restored with minimal disruption. Utilizing QuickBooks' built-in backup features or integrating external backup solutions into the workflow safeguards against data-related errors and their potential repercussions.

In a networked or cloud-based QuickBooks environment, strong network security protocols are indispensable. This involves secure, stable internet connections, effective firewalls, and safeguards against external threats. A secure network environment minimizes the risk of connectivity-related errors and protects financial data from potential security breaches.

Regular financial health checks and internal audits using QuickBooks can preempt many potential errors. This involves scrutinizing transaction records, reconciling accounts, and identifying irregularities or inconsistencies in the financial data. Regular audits can catch potential errors early on, allowing for timely corrective measures before the issues escalate.

Complex workflows and convoluted financial practices are often breeding grounds for errors in QuickBooks. Streamlining these workflows and simplifying financial processes can significantly mitigate the risk of errors. Standardizing data entry procedures, employing consistent accounting methods, and maintaining clear financial categorizations are key to reducing error risks.

QuickBooks itself offers a plethora of tools and features designed to prevent errors. From automated data entry to error-checking algorithms and diagnostic tools, effectively leveraging these features can significantly reduce the incidence of errors. For example, QuickBooks' automated reconciliation features can help avert common reconciliation errors, and its diagnostic tools can identify and rectify potential data file issues.

In conclusion, a proactive approach to preventing errors in QuickBooks is essential for businesses operating in the competitive and fast-paced American market. This approach is not merely a best practice but a fundamental strategy for ensuring operational efficiency and financial accuracy. By fostering a culture of continuous learning, maintaining regular software updates, implementing strong data backup and security protocols, conducting routine financial audits, simplifying financial workflows, and fully utilizing QuickBooks' preventive tools, businesses can significantly reduce the likelihood of errors. This proactive stance on error prevention ensures not just the smooth functioning of financial operations but also contributes to the overall resilience and adaptability of the business in a constantly evolving economic landscape.

Chapter 15: QuickBooks Shortcuts and Hacks

Navigating the world of finance with QuickBooks offers businesses a blend of precision, efficiency, and adaptability. In a landscape where time is a valued asset, knowing the intricacies of QuickBooks can propel a company's financial management to new heights. This chapter delves into the realm of shortcuts and hacks within QuickBooks, revealing ways to enhance productivity and streamline processes. From keyboard shortcuts that offer swift navigation to time-saving tips that simplify routine tasks, and the art of customizing QuickBooks to fit a business's unique requirements, this exploration is a journey towards mastering the software. It's about transforming QuickBooks from a tool into a tailored financial companion, one that aligns seamlessly with the rhythms of modern American business.

Keyboard Shortcuts

In the bustling world of American business, where efficiency and time management are not just valued but essential, QuickBooks stands as a vital ally for many companies. However, even within this framework of efficiency, there are hidden avenues and shortcuts that can further streamline financial management tasks. The first of these are keyboard shortcuts – a set of keystrokes that act like hidden passageways, allowing users to navigate QuickBooks with swiftness and precision.

Keyboard shortcuts in QuickBooks are more than just time-savers; they are the little efficiencies that, when added up, can significantly speed up routine tasks, leaving more time for strategic business activities. Imagine the daily accumulation of seconds and minutes saved by using a simple key combination instead of navigating through menus and options. This efficiency is especially crucial in the fast-paced American market, where the tempo of business demands quick yet accurate financial management.

For instance, consider the simple act of creating a new invoice – a frequent task for many businesses. Instead of reaching for the mouse, navigating through the menu, and selecting the option to create a new invoice, a simple press of 'Ctrl + I' in QuickBooks accomplishes the same task in a fraction of the time. Similarly, 'Ctrl + F' swiftly opens the search function, allowing users to quickly locate specific transactions or records without the need for tedious scrolling or menu navigation.

Navigating the dates in QuickBooks is another area where keyboard shortcuts shine. Rather than manually entering or selecting dates, shortcuts like '+' (plus key) to move forward a day and '-' (minus key) to move back a day can expedite data entry. For those dealing with financial data that spans weeks, months, or years, this simple hack can be a significant time-saver.

QuickBooks users frequently find themselves navigating between different sections of the software. Here, keyboard shortcuts act as rapid transit links, connecting various parts of QuickBooks with minimal effort. 'Ctrl + W' quickly opens the Write Checks window, and 'Ctrl + J' opens the Customer Center. These shortcuts allow users to jump from one task to another seamlessly, enhancing productivity and workflow fluidity.

Reconciliation, a critical but sometimes time-consuming task, can also benefit from these shortcuts. Pressing 'Ctrl + R' opens the reconcile window, setting the stage for a quick review of accounts. This is particularly beneficial for businesses that perform regular reconciliations to maintain accurate and up-to-date financial records.

Even navigating through the registers within QuickBooks can be expedited with shortcuts. 'Ctrl + Register' opens the register for the first account in your Chart of Accounts, allowing for rapid access and data entry. It's a simple yet effective way to quickly view transactions in specific accounts without multiple clicks.

Customization is another area where keyboard shortcuts play a significant role. While QuickBooks offers a range of customization options to suit various business needs, knowing the shortcuts to access these customization features can save time and enhance user experience. For example, 'Ctrl + P' opens the print dialog, a shortcut that is invaluable when customizing the printing of checks, reports, or invoices.

So, keyboard shortcuts in QuickBooks are more than just keystrokes; they are a gateway to enhanced productivity and efficiency. They embody the philosophy of working smarter, not harder, a mantra that resonates strongly in the American business ethos. By mastering these shortcuts, QuickBooks users can navigate the software with greater speed and ease, freeing up valuable time to focus on broader business strategies and goals. In an environment where time is a precious commodity, these keyboard shortcuts are not just hacks; they are essential tools for financial management efficiency.

Time-Saving Tips

In the competitive landscape of American business, where efficiency equates to success, QuickBooks emerges as more than just an accounting tool. It's a catalyst for productivity, offering a wealth of time-saving tips and tricks that, when employed adeptly, can transform the financial management of any business. These hacks are not just shortcuts; they are the keys to unlocking a more streamlined, effective approach to accounting – a necessity in today's fast-paced market.

The core of QuickBooks' time-saving utility lies in mastering efficient data entry. One of the most significant time drains in accounting is manually inputting transactional data. QuickBooks brilliantly counters this with features like batch entry capabilities and direct transaction import options. Importing bank and credit card transactions directly into QuickBooks, for instance, slashes the hours spent on manual data entry, simultaneously reducing the risk of human error and ensuring a smoother flow of financial information.

Customizable templates stand out as another potent feature in QuickBooks. The recurring nature of financial transactions in business necessitates a tool that can handle repetitiveness with ease. QuickBooks' customizable templates for invoices, purchase orders, and other recurring documents mean that once a template is set up to match a business's specific requirements, the creation of these documents becomes a matter of a few clicks. This functionality not only saves precious time but also brings consistency and professionalism to a business's financial documentation.

The often-tedious task of reconciliation is given a makeover in QuickBooks. Its reconciliation module simplifies matching bank and credit card transactions with entries in the software. With features like auto-match, QuickBooks can swiftly identify potential matches, reducing the manual effort required to a simple confirmation task. This kind of automation in reconciliation is a game-changer, especially for businesses that deal with a high volume of transactions.

Reporting, an indispensable yet time-consuming aspect of business, is made more efficient in QuickBooks through the ability to schedule automatic report generation and delivery. This feature is invaluable for businesses that rely on regular financial reports such as monthly sales or expense summaries. Automating this process means timely financial insights are available with minimal input, ensuring businesses can stay informed without constant manual intervention.

QuickBooks also offers a variety of navigation shortcuts within the software itself. The QuickBooks Toolbar, for instance, can be customized with shortcuts to the most frequently used functions or reports, functioning like a personalized control panel. This setup provides instant access to key areas of the software, cutting down on navigation time and boosting overall productivity.

The initial setup and customization of QuickBooks are also pivotal in optimizing its efficiency. A setup that mirrors the specific needs and nuances of a business can save considerable time down the line. From tailoring the chart of accounts to configuring the software's preferences, these initial steps lay the groundwork for a more streamlined and relevant accounting experience.

For users of QuickBooks Online, automation extends even further. The platform's capabilities for setting up automatic invoice reminders, recurring billing, and auto-categorizing bank transactions mean that many routine tasks can be set to operate autonomously. This level of automation frees up businesses to focus on higher-level financial strategy and decision-making.

So, the array of time-saving tips and hacks in QuickBooks is a treasure trove for businesses seeking to enhance their financial management efficiency. In an economic environment where time is a valuable currency, these features are not just conveniences; they are essential tools that enable businesses to stay agile, informed, and ahead of the competition. Mastering these aspects of QuickBooks allows businesses not only to save time but also to harness their financial data more effectively, leading to smarter, more strategic business decisions.

Customizing QuickBooks

In the diverse and ever-evolving landscape of American business, QuickBooks stands as a versatile and powerful tool, integral to the financial management of countless enterprises. Yet, its true potency is unlocked not merely through its inherent features but through its capacity for customization. This ability to tailor QuickBooks to the unique operational rhythms and specific needs of a business transforms it from a standard accounting software into a bespoke financial management solution, offering a strategic edge in efficiency and effectiveness.

Customization in QuickBooks is akin to crafting a finely-tuned instrument, specifically designed to harmonize with the unique financial melody of a business. It involves adjusting and refining the software to align precisely with a company's specific accounting practices, reporting requirements, and operational workflows. When QuickBooks is customized, every feature and function is molded to serve a specific, strategic purpose, enhancing both the efficiency and efficacy of financial management.

Consider the dashboard, the nerve center of QuickBooks, which presents a snapshot of the business's financial health. Customizing the dashboard to display the most pertinent information immediately upon login can significantly streamline daily operations. For instance, a business that prioritizes cash flow management might customize the dashboard to prominently display cash flow trends and key receivables. This immediate access to critical data accelerates decision-making and ensures that important financial metrics are always at the forefront.

The power of QuickBooks also lies in its robust reporting capabilities, and customizing these reports to reflect the specific needs of a business can yield profound insights. Custom reports can be tailored to focus on the most relevant data, whether it's tracking specific expense categories, monitoring project profitability, or dissecting sales trends. These tailored reports offer a deeper, more nuanced view of the business's financial landscape, enabling data-driven decision-making with greater precision and confidence.

Another facet of QuickBooks' customization is the ability to streamline workflows through tailored forms and templates. By customizing these documents to include necessary fields, company branding, and specific layouts, businesses can ensure consistency and professionalism across all financial documentation. This extends to invoices, purchase orders, sales receipts, and more, ensuring that every financial document aligns with the business's specific processes and brand identity.

QuickBooks also offers the capability to automate routine tasks through customized rules and alerts. For example, businesses can set rules for automatically categorizing bank transactions, which QuickBooks will diligently apply, thereby saving time and reducing manual effort. Custom alerts can be configured to notify when important financial thresholds are reached or deadlines approach, ensuring critical financial matters receive timely attention.

In a multi-user QuickBooks environment, tailoring user access and permissions is crucial for both operational efficiency and data security. Customizing user roles ensures that each team member has access to the tools and information they need for their specific role while safeguarding sensitive financial data. This targeted approach to user permissions not only enhances security but also streamlines workflow, ensuring that employees are focused and unencumbered by extraneous data or features.

The integration capability of QuickBooks further accentuates its customizability. By seamlessly integrating with a variety of other business tools and platforms – from CRM systems to e-commerce platforms – QuickBooks can become a central component of a broader business ecosystem. This integration fosters a unified workflow across various business functions, enhancing overall operational efficiency and data coherence.

In concluding this exploration of QuickBooks shortcuts and hacks, it becomes evident that QuickBooks is more than just accounting software; it's a platform ripe with possibilities for enhanced efficiency and customization. The journey through its shortcuts, time-saving tips, and customization options illuminates how businesses can fine-tune their financial operations. By embracing these aspects, companies can unlock the full potential of QuickBooks, turning it into a bespoke tool that not only addresses their financial needs but also complements their unique business strategies. This mastery of QuickBooks shortcuts and hacks is not just about working faster; it's about working smarter, ensuring that businesses stay agile, informed, and ahead in the competitive American marketplace.

Appendices

Glossary of Terms

In the intricate tapestry of business finance, where jargon and technical terms often weave a complex web, understanding the language is crucial. This glossary of terms, an essential appendix to the world of QuickBooks and accounting, serves as a compass to navigate through the often convoluted terminologies used in daily financial management. It's not just a list of definitions; it's a bridge connecting the uninitiated to the core concepts of accounting and QuickBooks functionality, a tool to demystify the language of finance and make it accessible to all.

Accounting Period: This term refers to a specific time frame for which financial records and reports are prepared. It's the canvas on which the financial story of a business is painted, typically spanning a month, quarter, or year. Understanding the accounting period is crucial in interpreting financial reports and performance metrics accurately.

Balance Sheet: Imagine a snapshot capturing a moment in the life of a business, showing what it owns (assets) and owes (liabilities), along with the equity invested by the owners at a specific point in time. The balance sheet does just that, offering a glimpse into the financial stability and health of a business.

Chart of Accounts: This term refers to the backbone of a business's financial record-keeping system. It's a categorized list of all accounts used in the general ledger, including assets, liabilities, equity, revenue, and expenses. It's like a map guiding users through the terrain of a company's financial transactions.

Depreciation: In the world of business finance, assets like equipment and vehicles lose value over time. Depreciation is the method of allocating the cost of these tangible assets over their useful lives. It's a way of recognizing that assets contribute to revenue generation over several years, not just at the point of purchase.

Equity: Think of equity as a business's net worth. It's the residual interest in the assets of the business after deducting liabilities. In simpler terms, it's what the business owners truly own – their stake in the company after all debts are paid.

General Ledger: This term is akin to the grand diary of a business's financial transactions. The general ledger records all the financial details of a company's activities, serving as a central repository for accounting data transferred from all sub-ledgers and journals.

Liquidity: In the financial world, liquidity is about accessibility. It refers to how quickly and easily assets can be converted into cash, a crucial factor for meeting a business's short-term obligations. High liquidity means a business can quickly turn assets into cash without losing value.

Profit and Loss Statement (P&L): Also known as an income statement, this document is a financial report that shows revenues, expenses, and profits or losses over a specific period. It tells the story of a business's operational efficiency and profitability, providing insights into how well the business is performing in generating profit.

Reconciliation: Imagine the act of ensuring two sets of records (usually the balances of two accounts) are in agreement. Reconciliation in accounting is just that – it's the process of ensuring that figures from financial records match those from bank statements, for instance.

Vendor: In QuickBooks and general accounting, a vendor is any individual or company that provides goods or services to your business. They are key players in the business ecosystem, impacting everything from inventory to accounts payable.

This glossary serves as more than just a reference; it's a guide through the language of finance and accounting, a tool to empower users of QuickBooks and other financial management tools. Understanding these terms is crucial in navigating the financial landscape, enabling business owners, managers, and employees to converse fluently in the language of finance, and thus make informed, strategic decisions.

Glossary of Terms

In the world of financial management, particularly within the realms of QuickBooks, the journey of mastering the software and navigating the nuances of accounting is an ongoing one. The path is lined with a myriad of resources and tools, each designed to enhance understanding, efficiency, and proficiency. This appendix, dedicated to additional resources and tools, is not just a compilation of aids; it's a curated selection designed to bolster the journey of any QuickBooks user, from novices to seasoned professionals, in the varied and vibrant landscape of American business.

Comprehensive Online Forums and Communities

The digital age has blessed us with online communities – forums where like-minded individuals converge to discuss, debate, and disseminate information. For QuickBooks users, these forums are invaluable. Websites such as the Intuit Community and QuickBooks Users offer a platform for users to ask questions, share experiences, and gain insights from peers and experts alike. Here, a treasure trove of information awaits, from troubleshooting common issues to sharing advanced usage tips.

Educational Webinars and Tutorials

In the pursuit of knowledge, the role of webinars and tutorials cannot be overstated. QuickBooks offers a range of webinars – both live and recorded – that cover various aspects of the software. These sessions, led by experts, provide deep dives into specific features, updates, and best practices. Additionally, platforms like YouTube host a multitude of video tutorials, catering to all levels of QuickBooks proficiency.

Books and Guides

For those who prefer the tangible feel of a book or the structured approach of a guide, there are numerous publications on QuickBooks. These range from official guides published by Intuit to works by independent accounting experts. These books often provide step-by-step instructions, practical examples, and tips to enhance the user experience. Titles like "QuickBooks for Dummies" offer an accessible entry point for beginners, while more advanced guides delve into the software's more complex capabilities.

QuickBooks Training and Certification Programs

For individuals seeking a more formalized learning structure, QuickBooks training and certification programs are an excellent resource. These programs, offered by Intuit and other certified educators, provide comprehensive training on various aspects of QuickBooks. Upon completion, certifications serve as a testament to the user's proficiency, a valuable asset in the professional world.

Customized Business Consulting Services

Sometimes, the most effective learning comes through personalized guidance. Many businesses opt for customized consulting services where QuickBooks experts provide tailored advice and solutions. These services can range from basic setup and training to in-depth financial analysis and reporting strategies, depending on the business's specific needs.

Integrative Tools and Applications

In an era where business software is expected to be versatile and integrative, QuickBooks does not disappoint. A plethora of integrative tools and applications are available that work seamlessly with QuickBooks, enhancing its functionality. These include apps for inventory management, time tracking, payroll services, and CRM systems. Leveraging these tools can significantly expand QuickBooks' capabilities, turning it into a comprehensive business management solution.

Government and Educational Resources

Lastly, governmental and educational institutions often provide resources beneficial to QuickBooks users. The IRS website, for instance, offers guidelines on accounting standards and tax compliance which are crucial for proper financial management. Educational institutions and business schools frequently publish research and articles on accounting best practices and software utilization, providing a more academic perspective on financial management tools.

In conclusion, this array of additional resources and tools for QuickBooks users is a testament to the software's expansive role in the world of finance and business management. From online communities and educational webinars to formal training programs and integrative applications, these resources cater to a wide spectrum of needs and learning styles. Harnessing these tools effectively can significantly enhance a user's experience with QuickBooks, providing them with the knowledge, skills, and confidence to navigate the complexities of financial management in the fast-paced and ever-evolving American business landscape.

Frequently Asked Questions

In the landscape of QuickBooks, where complex financial management is distilled into a user-friendly interface, questions inevitably arise. Users, ranging from novices in small startups to seasoned professionals in established businesses, encounter queries as they navigate through the software's multitude of features. This Frequently Asked Questions section serves not just as a repository of answers but as a guide through the common curiosities and challenges encountered in QuickBooks. It's a compilation born out of real-world usage, reflecting the collective experiences and inquiries of a diverse user base.

1. How Can I Customize My QuickBooks for Specific Business Needs?

Customization is a cornerstone of QuickBooks' appeal. Users can tailor almost every aspect of their experience, from setting up a personalized dashboard to customizing forms and reports. This involves adjusting the settings under the 'Preferences' menu, where you can define how you want QuickBooks to handle things like invoices, expenses, payroll, and taxes. For more specific needs, QuickBooks also supports various add-ons and integrations, allowing businesses to connect other tools and services they use for a seamless financial management experience.

2. What Are the Best Practices for Data Backup and Security in QuickBooks?

Protecting financial data is paramount. QuickBooks provides several tools and features to ensure data security. Regular backups, either through the software or using a third-party service, are essential. It's advisable to set a routine for backups, ensuring they are done consistently. For security, QuickBooks offers features like password protections, encrypted data, and multi-factor authentication. Keeping the software updated is also critical, as each update often includes security enhancements.

3. How Can I Efficiently Manage Cash Flow in QuickBooks?

Cash flow management is vital for any business. QuickBooks helps track cash flow in real-time, providing insights into current financial standings. Utilizing the 'Cash Flow Projector' tool within QuickBooks gives a forward-looking view, helping predict future cash flow based on existing data. Regularly monitoring accounts receivable and payable through QuickBooks and setting up invoice reminders can also aid in maintaining healthy cash flow.

4. What Should I Do If I Encounter an Error in QuickBooks?

Encountering errors can be frustrating, but QuickBooks offers several resources for troubleshooting. The first step is to understand the error message – QuickBooks provides a description for most errors. For more complex issues, the QuickBooks support website, community forums, or contacting a QuickBooks certified professional can provide solutions. Regular software updates can also prevent many common errors.

5. How Do I Integrate QuickBooks with Other Business Tools?

Integration expands QuickBooks' functionality, allowing it to work in tandem with other business tools. QuickBooks offers a range of integrations with popular business software for CRM, e-commerce, payroll, and more. These integrations can usually be found and set up within the 'Apps' section in QuickBooks. It's important to ensure that the other software versions are compatible with your QuickBooks version for seamless integration.

6. Can I Use QuickBooks for Tax Preparation and Filing?

Yes, QuickBooks can significantly streamline tax preparation and filing. It organizes all financial data needed for tax purposes, simplifies the tracking of deductible expenses, and can integrate with tax software. QuickBooks also keeps up with the latest tax rates and regulations to ensure accuracy. For businesses with more complex tax situations, it's advisable to consult with a tax professional.

7. What Is the Best Way to Use QuickBooks for Payroll?

QuickBooks offers a robust payroll feature, which can be fully integrated into your financial management workflow. The software can handle payroll calculations, tax withholdings, payroll tax filings, and direct deposits. Setting up payroll in QuickBooks involves entering detailed company, employee, and tax information. Staying compliant with payroll laws and regulations is crucial, and QuickBooks helps by providing regular updates and reminders.

In summary, this Frequently Asked Questions section provides a glimpse into the common queries that arise among QuickBooks users, offering solutions and guidance that enhance the overall software experience. Whether it's tackling technical challenges, optimizing financial management processes, or leveraging QuickBooks' vast capabilities, these questions and answers serve as a valuable resource, guiding users to harness the full potential of QuickBooks in their business endeavors.

43212474R00105